C0036 09824

CW00496396

the 1960s *the*

orange sunshine

Jeremy Reed

'Jeremy Reed uses words the way most of us use our lungs. Except they are much more precious, and every breath is a wondrous revelation.'

Mark Simpson

'Enfolding, disturbing, mesmerically filmic, *Orange Sunshine* is nothing less than the verse portrait of an epoch. It brings to vivid life the many troubled, exuberant, doomed, contradictory, inspirational phenomena which comprised the drug-sodden, determinedly enquiring, narcissistic, perilously seductive underground culture of the mythic 1960s. In its detail and ambition alone, therefore, *Orange Sunshine* confirms Reed's place as a great lyric poet of pop's shadow.'

Michael Bracewell

'Where David Bailey's black & white photographs captured the stylish and selfconscious surface appearance of the pop stars, fashionistas, artists and gangsters of the sixties, Jeremy Reed's take on the same range of cultural icons from that decade probes deep into the mindset and brings the fizzing creativity of the period to life more powerfully, truthfully and succinctly than any academic or journalistic commentator has yet managed.

Having consistently embraced the energy and atmosphere of the glamorous, vibrant, casually decadent and alluringly sexual aspects of popular culture and especially rock music as a gloriously improper subject for his luscious and intense poetry, Reed—in looking back at the formative influences of his adolescence—immerses the reader in an intoxicating epic journey back to a time when style and substance were briefly and joyously entwined.'

Marco Livingstone

the 1960s *the party that lasted a decade*

orange sunshine

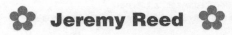 **Jeremy Reed**

S·A·F

**Glasgow City Council
Cultural & Leisure Services
Libraries Info.& Learning
A**

C6003609824	
Askews	16-Aug-2006
821.914 L⊤	£8.99

First edition. First printing.
First published in 2006
by SAF Publishing

SAF Publishing Ltd.
149 Wakeman Road
London. NW10 5BH
ENGLAND

email: info@safpublishing.com
www.safpublishing.com

ISBN 10: 0 946719 88 8
ISBN 13: 978 0 946719 88 4

Text copyright © 2006 Jeremy Reed.
The right of Jeremy Reed to be identified as the author of this work
has been asserted by him in accordance with the Copyright, Designs
and Patents Act, 1988.

All rights reserved. No part of this publication may be transmitted in
any form, or by any means, electronic, photocopying, recording or
otherwise, without the prior permission of the publisher.

Cover images: Moon Landing: © 2006 Jupiter Images Corporation
                  Rolling Stones: David Farrell/Redferns
                  Demonstration: Michael Ochs Archives/Redferns
                  Kennedy: © 2006 Jupiter Images Corporation
                  Bomb: © 2006 Jupiter Images Corporation

In some cases it has not proved possible to ascertain or trace original
illustration copyright holders, and the publishers would be grateful to
hear from the photographers concerned.
All lyrics quoted are for review, study or critical purposes.

A CIP catalogue record for this book is available from
the British Library.

Printed in England by The Cromwell Press, Trowbridge, Wiltshire.

For
Lene Rasmussen, John Robinson
and Stephen Andrews

'When one is young, summer records define your life.
Later they explain it.'

Andrew Loog Oldham *2 Stoned*

'Part of the job of the imagination is to remind us of the
marvellous...'

J.G. Ballard (interviewed 1983)

'Nobody approaches the customer to ask them what they want.
The assistants are all in casual clothes—in the case of the Mod
Male in very Mod clothes. They just smoke and lean against
the wall and put records on... It's all very casual.'

John Stephen

Contents

MODS AND CELEBRITIES

SHOPPING

1966 ON POETRY'S TRAIL

ON THE BEACH

MEMO FROM TURNER

LSD

CALIFORNIA DREAMING

CHARLIE'S HEX ON SHARON TATE

GIMME SHELTER

BRAIN DAMAGE

POSTCRIPT: TROPICAL DISEASE 1970s

MY GENERATION

ORANGE SUNSHINE

Crawdaddy 1963

They cut it hot: its one-shoulder-striptease,
the singer's sweater angled girlishly
each time he slows the tempo to a drawl

and sees his image on the mirrored wall
as someone else grown dangerous with power,
a stalker talking blues with maracas,

a dervish improvising a stage prowl.
It's Brian's blues harp shimmers between riffs
creating colours with impromptu speed,

as though each blue demands a variant,
a grey or mauve as textured subtlety.
The drummer's three piece suit citifies rock

and contrasts with Keith's wolfishly unkempt
appropriation of a waistcoat, jeans,
his Bo Diddley chords so naively tight

they parrot source, but come out garagey.
The crowd's on burn, new blood alive
to a youth gestalt: they are on their knees

instinctively caught up by the tempo,
conflicting factions finding unity
in gestural dance, raw-sexed abandonment

to poppy R&B—the leather boys
dancing with Mods, all warring archetypes
dissolved in a collective energy

at Station Road, the Thames windowing ice,
the singer reinventing masculinity
with pouty, sexless contempt, winning all

by blowing losers clean out of the door,
the rhythm fast, untiring, and the charge
creating the 60s on a dance floor.

John Lennon (Early)

A roostertail pompadour
licked on a Scouse iconoclast
oiled in black leather

in the neon-jumpy Reeperbahn;
his wit turns like the Mersey
sorting undertow flotsam.

His spiky irreverence
rocks at the Indra Club like the Führer
staging agitprop dementia.

Blood fizzed by lager,
he guns belligerent rhythm
at Hamburg goose-steppers,

his past like a black pool
sucking him under
in whorls of treacle.

Once there was childhood
and swinging out on a taut rope
in front of a double-decker

on a suicide pendulum,
the gamble like Russian roulette,
recklessly Dostoevskian.

Now exiled and angular
he turns up the ante
on snarling decibels.

He's a small club lemon
sniffing bigger horizons,
an unrepentant Liverpudlian

self conscious in glasses,
sniffing the port, the red light district,
stacked boot heels worn flat, but sure of his vision.

Edith Grove

The fungi on the walls are like blue bread,
fist-sized excrescences, crop-circle whorls,
paisley blotches abseiling to the bed.

Mick's gone off with a satchel bricked with books,
the two guitarists strum with cold fingers
to old guttural Muddy Waters hooks.

They poncho blankets. A red winter sun
squeezes an orange over Chelsea docks.
Brian does slide, a riffy trick he's won.

Andrew's in town at Strickland's Record Store,
corner of Dean and Compton, riffling sounds;
the future thumps him like the subway roar.

Soho's all putzah. Johnny Danger's floor's
the third one up. A pink shirt says it all.
It signals access to fire-proofed doors.

Back in the Chelsea den, they cut it raw.
Keith's understudy Buddy Holly licks
break through the jamming like a sudden thaw.

The dishes tower like a Westway high-rise,
a scissored NME rafts on the floor,
small ads circled. Mick's make-up's a surprise—

Max Factor eye-shadows, a blue, a green
left open on the basin, Quant powder
skid-marking the rim with a dusty sheen…

Nobody loves you when you're down and out.
The heating's disconnected, room's a tip,
the mess providing the rebellious clout

to foster image—spotty bad boy loons,
defiant, dead broke, stealing guitar picks
and quickly mastering Bo Diddley tunes.

1964
NOT FADE AWAY

Rainy Day Hits

He's wide-eyed 1964,
Bob Dylan toking verbal hits,
trancing the drug's autonomy
and free-associating words
like an improvised mantra

dovetailed to marijuana,
a song scrambled from scrolling smoke.
The new decade invents itself
like vertebrae along his spine.
He rolls New York into a joint,

inhales the city, reconstructs
his origins inside a point
that glowers with a feeding match.
His raw poetry brings it home—
the shaman's oracular pour

from acrid weed, a lexicon
of knee-jerking non sequiturs,
image collisions jabbed at hot
into a notebook, then rephrased
under cold sober Woodstock skies,

the rain bringing him down again,
he does 'Mr. Tambourine Man' clear
as a fish stroking water.
Bathtub amphetamine's the speed
he crafts on, pushes 'Eight Miles High'

into stratospheric wobble.
He's protest in a sugar cube,
the rainbow compressed in its molecules:
bikes it out to his band's pink house,
cooks secrets in the basement.

Bob's the inspirational avatar
of black shades cool, keeps to the hills,
stalking his inspiration like a deer,
smelling its blood and seeing words
written by angels on its side.

Andrew Loog Oldham

Skinny, entrepreneurial zeitgeist,
ex-Epstein, ex-Quant
window dresser, aka Sandy Beach
and Chancery Lane,
names like the feather boa swish
of drag artistes at the Vauxhall Tavern:
blown away at the Crawdaddy
by Jagger's explosive bi-itch,
the Stones' lean-mean attitude
in wiring rock to R&B,
burnt on the moment by their flash
and fielding it as manager,
twitchy in pink hexagonal lenses
and studied eyeliner,
match-mate to Mick's lashed mascara,
rounding up the band's energies
to corral them at Decca,
work on their bad boy lowlife sneer
through Jagger's affected cockney,
hustle for crowd hysteria
to detonate each smashed up show,
moved into Mapesbury Road with Mick
and Chrissie Shrimpton, shared his bed
and make-up and camp repartee,
wrote liner notes surreal as bleach
turned a-syntactical purple,
sold out to Allen Klein, the deal
haemorrhaging profit,
got fried, then wiped by ECT,
a green-lighter disorbiting
in conflagratory mania,
booted into redundancy
like strawberry-haired Brian Jones,
a hard fall, over, under,
sideways, down and out corridor,
a decade-shaper exiting
like a burnt-out meteor.

Reg King

Reg bangs a blue Chevy convertible
wrong side of the road across town,
his wall-eyed gofer's handgun stare
fixed on a rainy Shaftesbury Avenue,
The 'Butcher King', pet criminal
to Andrew Oldham, sings in falsetto
Eeney meeney miney moe
suck a cock
and break a toe

take no prisoners in Soho.
His broadcloth-blue tab-collar shirt mirrors
his herringbone jacketed employer's,
both wear skinny black woollen ties
sharper than a gangster's.

Reg slams up outside De Hems,
the Ronettes crowding on the stereo
with run mascara conviction
underlined by a Phil Spector scherzo.
Eeney meeney miney moe
give me head I'll let you go,
money wallpapers a fist

cemented to a limp wrist.
Reg's role-model's Ronnie Kray—
shoot and you forget who they were
pillared beneath a motorway?

A black and white frames him in Trafalgar Square,
circa 1964, sharp-suited,
a blonde ruffle in sandy hair,
the National Portrait Gallery backdropped
in grainy resolution, (a grey day?)—
his smile committed to the upbeat plot
of living dangerously and closeted,
while the Stones ride high on 'Not Fade Away'.

Regent Sound

A boxy hotel room-sized studio,
stripped ivory paint, the burnt omelette blotches
rashing the walls; a demo-space
in Denmark Street, mono only
for primitives—the Stones in there
bleeding their amps to wall of noise.

The red-haired, tie-thin Dadaist
impresario—ALO—
works the control room like a test pilot,
the accidental and the found
mixed at a level that's so raw
it detonates ear-drums.

The sounds live and direct-to-disc,
a cobbled blues-punk, teeny rip,
a sonic speedball like a Tyson fist
mashing the gobsmacked Decca head,
a spotty, in your nose, dude-bravura
breaking taboos like digging up the dead.

Jagger's a fire-eating mike-swallower
surfing his breath into the song,
needling it with subjective fangs.
They leak delay into an in-house theme,
a customised state-of-the-art motif.
Small money. Big time. An art student's dream.

Egg boxes for sound baffling, they plug in,
extemporise round an acoustic riff,
then kick a blues storm through 'Not Fade Away'.
The B-side's nailed in twenty minutes flat—
'Little by Little' with its twelve-bar blues
and churlish vocals from a lip curled cat.

They can the songs on credit, pool cab fares,
leave scuff marks from their blue Anello boots,
their moment coming, like they've grown with it
as destiny, a welling up of roots
to meet the age—they take it in their stride—
and notch up a decade of blazing hits.

Dressed to Kill (Andrew Oldham)

Austin's on Shaftesbury Avenue
for catchlight window-shopping, button-downs
in grey and blue denim, reversible
hounds tooth jackets with staggered vents—
the black and white and chocolatey
with ochre, as the day's event,

or a blue herringbone, its grainy knit
like zigzag epidermis. Post-rush hour
he reviews Sportique on Old Compton Street,
white hipsters, fey crochet, green angora,
details to a gay lifestyle,
and saves a month for a black knitted tie

from John Michaels, adds a blue gingham shirt,
fly-fronted, tab-collared, a distinct splash
of hip identity, strafes through the racks
of C&A's for the anomalous—
a one off bottle-green mohair suit,
the oyster lining flash with paisley swirls,

a statement of cutting-edge pill-head youth
doing style off a gloss Chess records sleeve,
diversifying with a strawberry
Vince shirt, or John Stephen's hipsters,
so crotch-level risqué, they're scandalous,
compact grape-bunches forcing at the seams…

He smells the moment, like geraniums
come up after rain on a summer's day,
maximum potential, the upbeat swing
linked to the music, a black R&B,
sharp as the fashion, hot as paprika,
cooking a loud groove in a London yard.

His make-up's like a peachy permatan,
a shine on being vulnerable. He sights
his tie's lapsed Adam's-apple, bumps it up,
gets wolf-whistled, stonewalled at a bus-stop,
ruffles his bottle-red hair, picks up pace
and hustles like he lives, catch as catch can.

44/46 Maddox Street

A fourth floor spare room quango
of druggy lateral
head-games—
two bi-polars—Oldham, Meaden,
psyching into gangster spin
doing polypharmacy
from a brightly coloured stash
wowed inside a chocolate-box.
Meaden's into aliens
and buried lakes—they're twelve miles deep—
iced over on Jupiter's moon
Europa. Meaden sells the Who
as a prototype Mod High Numbers
and sips bottled blue water
from WI Europa.
He seems to disconnect from gravity
and part company with his chair.
Oldham's the Stones' hard sell
rogue cell
self-promoting oracle;
the king of flash on Soho's patch,
danger in motion, squally red—
haired quantum-leaper
using hype like a graffito
nailing gimmicks to the wall.
He's the grand Guignol with the two-tone blue Chevy,
window floored on the pavement side,
whacking the unsuspecting,
face crumpled with explosive laughter.
Overkill's his natural tempo—
up the beat and up the beat
to optimal crescendo;
Reg the chauffeur bending risk
to a straight line: Oldham in a black cloak
jumping out at the lights, doing bat wings
to lift the scarlet lining.

Chess Studios 1964

Muddy Waters paints the ceiling
menthol-green, odd-jobbing slashes
like a naïve emulsioned
Barnett Newman,
shafts a brush in the can.

Charlie's sniffing through the archives
for legendary Chess
45s.
Bill requisitions memorabilia.
Brian slyly sips Wild Turkey.

Five British ingénues
whoop it up in Ron Malo's room,
unnerved by the sound's sharp creases
moptop cowed blues parvenus
cracking through 'Under the Boardwalk',

summery as ripening lemons,
Keith cranks proto-power chords
and loping tangential figures
on Chicago misogyny
a captious 'It's All Over Now',

canned to commandeer the hotspot
as a global No 1.
Muddy drops in, blotched by green blobs
splashed on his dark glasses,
listens gobsmacked to bottleneck

on 'I Can't Be Satisfied'
magicked by the Cheltenham
maestro,
blonde fringe patterned like macramé.
Mick's the part in hounds tooth hipsters,

melismatic tone role-searching
for a viable persona
Cockney slut, intransigent
gigolo, or whisky-shot
Arkansas sharecropper.

Al Capone's office opposite
reinforces legend
South Michigan Avenue
catching fire in windy sunlight
from a sky curved greeny-blue,

Chuck Berry dropping by to sell
his itchy standards and applaud
Mick's vocal swagger, instructing
their take on covers, 'play it lean
and tight and let the rhythm swing.'

American Tour 1964

The highway's longer than Proust's novel,
Route 66 telescopes
like Napoleon
into Russia.
It's like crossing the sky's curve

and stopping off between planets.
A red Chevy eats the road
stereo blasting
Otis Redding.
Brian's six calla lily stems

are heavier than golf clubs
on his black elephant cord lap.
He's a strawberry blonde bobbed
like Audrey Hepburn
carriers stacked up with Stax

and Motown vinyl.
Their tour zeroes as it fans out,
boxy sound cubed in undersold
heat-prickly arenas.
Mick does fame dancing to himself

with mincy steps, as though his feet
are bandaged to retarded stubs
like a Chinese fetish.
His act's from the Vauxhall Tavern
travestying Diana Ross…

Backstage, the cops snout .44s
at Keith's up all night eyeballs,
flick his fringe with a baton.
They're roughed up on a gutsy haul,
Detroit, Pittsburgh, Cleveland, LA,

fetching up at Carnegie Hall,
brokering a mini-riot,
sweet success in the Big Apple,
a first bite, the juice so sharp
it burns like whisky from the bottle.

Kicking In 1964

90. The English summer spoils to drought.
London turns mirage, Hampshire's grizzled blonde
slashed by red poppies: everywhere the land

shoulders its raw defensives—dust and stone.
They're slammed across motorway gradients,
cooking assault on small towns, targeting

resistance with hormonal-soup,
slapping maracas to a muddy beat,
the voodoo-tempo working like a hex...

The hall at Plymouth's on impacted heat,
explosive tension layer by layer stripped down
to optimal hysterics, dementia

that surfs the crowd in pheromonal waves
peaking in a front row that surfs the stage,
chair legs ripped off as splintered weaponry...

The band do motions with their instruments,
their sound inaudible, their gestural quirks
suggesting counter-terrorists

doing Kabuki behind police helmets,
protected from the riot they incite,
by a bottled, beat-up constabulary:

each number ripped into dismemberment.
It's life and death, and they're prepared to run
at the first break in the blue barrier,

the first knife-in-the-teeth vengeful weirdo
whose girl loves Brian, and whose vaulting leap
projects him headfirst at the microphone.

Don't Bring Me Down—Pretty Things

Leathers the chin
abrasively. Street grit
in the delivery,
a cuffed stop and start R&B,
maracas sounding like hailstone bites

shaken over gravel.
They pin the song, and let it go,
chase off in pursuit,
stamp on it, forward and back
chase off again, as though heeling
a wobbly fireball

underfoot.
Nothing so in the face, the raw
squeezed like a lemon.
The vocal's smeared, it collects stains
like a tennis ball whacked
across forecourt.

A simple thing: a mean
complaint, is how it's phrased:
the put down winning back
a lick of pride: an arts-school grace
in hitting bottom,
but still saving face.

They lurch up-tempo, then slam dead
like a coach on a mountain road
shocked up against the boundary rail:
the tension so nuclear
inside the pause
it might explode.

Lands in the Top Ten, swipishly,
like the Krays walked in the door
with shooters raised.
Kicks with a feisty afterglow,
a sneered reminder they'll be back
raunchy with trouble, blow by blow.

The Merseybeats

The quiet ones, frock coats and frills,
'I Think of You' a ballady
snowball amongst strafed decibels,
a peppermint cream sound, tempo
dissolving like dark chocolate
on the tongue.
Their songs are love letters written by chords
stretched lazily the way a cat
compounds its yoga to a ball
of tabby somnolence. 'Don't Turn Around'
sleepwalks its way from Liverpool
to vamp the air-waves, frothy style
spilling lace on the charts.
They're soft like a blue velvet cuff,
tooling romance from dockside origins,
finding a way to reach the heart
and shape a song to settle there
as a red sequinned fit.
Their accent's thick as epitaph,
posted into the song like a ship's name
glowering above the harbour berth,
a vocal trademark.
'Wishin' and Hopin'' twinkles with regret,
as though love's better kept top shelf
like clear gold honey in a jar
sealed from the enquiring spoon.
Short-lived, un-adaptive to change,
they lost out, got jettisoned in dry-dock,
another act in pop's unending mortuary
of casualties—three hits a rocky end
the future sealed up like an envelope.

SCANDAL AND THE FIRM

Scandal Christine Keeler

She's leggy 18 with a showgirl's tease
    groomed at Murray's in Soho:
the diamond rings—25 caraters
    are gifts from Jack, (Jack Profumo).
She necks him at the Ritz: the waiter sees
    his hand by fugitive detours
take up position on her knees.

Her spike heels clatter outside Wimpole Mews,
    her osteopath pimp's recess
in a cobbled WI courtyard.
    He fires up the fizzy excess
with which she parties—Stephen Ward
    selling her body off to class
as London's hottest teeny news.

Mandy's her partner. Ward sits in a chair
    sketching Jack as he frisks the two
with a playful columnar libido.
    Eyes closed, half shot, he can't tell who is who
except the flounce of Christine's hair
    is livelier with a red twist
done for audacious dare.

Ward pops a cork. Another minister
    serves dinner naked, genuflects
in a pink sequinned mask and entertains
    by confessing how he infects
his partners compulsively—him or her
    with whatever new STD's
the monthly flavour.

Jamaican Johnny's got a sniff of Jack.
    He's Chrissie's lover and for free.
He's got to know the Jag, it's there Fridays
    its buffed black gloss sweating money.
He kneads a gun and keeps watch at the back
    on the lugubrious visitor
he intends to carjack.

Johnny's got drugs for Chrissie and he's mad
    she's harnessed to a man who's flash,
duplicitous and chauffeured to the yard
    pays for it with Coutts dispensed cash.
He's got a gun because he's had
    it up to here with being black
and mean and bad.

Jack alternates with Eugene Ivanov
    gifting her minks and caviar.
It's espionage. Ward snoops on Jack
    the suave ministerial philanderer.
Johnny thinks one's a Romanov.
    He has the photos. Ward's spy camera
framing each compromising move.

Johnny acts up and bullet-holes a tyre
    the reverb trapped in Harley Street,
the blast repeated and re-amplified.
    A cop breaks orbit from his beat
and wrestles Johnny before he can fire
    another shot to bring Jack out
disgraced, his hands raised in the air?

The Mews is raided. Jack resigns in shame.
    Ward ODs on white moon-shaped pills.
Chrissie goes under, when she drinks
    it's her own hand now that refills
the whiskey tumbler, and her name
    is vilified; the poison stings
and works its way out as a sort of fame.

The Firm (Ronnie Kray)

A snubby Mauser pistol on the bed—
it's Ronnie's cold prosthetic toy,
the chunky extension weighting his fist
a 9mm semi-automatic
liquidating all dialogue.
He thumbs a photo of a teeny boy

recruited from the Dilly scene,
bare torso and tightly packed bikini
exploiting his cool fantasy
of coming out with a blue rock
same-sex marriage to naïve spotty rent.
The thought pumps juice into his cock.

Sometimes he hears a voice, it's not his own,
demanding that he kills to bond
with someone deeper than reality.
He knew it once reviewing sides of beef
in Harrods Food Hall, gun in his pocket,
how doing mental killings brought relief

from feeding depression with gin.
His clammy hand aches to design impact,
the cool indifferent sort that wins applause
as brutally demonstrative,
a shoot out viewed by gangster witnesses
as a hard-headed psychopathic fact.

He's rich on scams from Esmerelda's Barn,
sharp-suited, bulked in Reggie's Cadillac—
its chrome trashy as the 8-carat ring
heisted for sovereign power on his fist.
Cornell's his target, a local gofer
who called him a fat poof with a limp wrist.

He's waited for this at the Blind Beggar,
his Mahler symphony or Beethoven,
walks in casual, (sights Cornell at the bar),
empties the gun three times into his head,
walks out into the Vallance Road a saint
the blood spot on his mohair shiny red.

The Firm (Reggie Kray)

A wide shouldered, double-breasted chalk stripe
Chicago style bespoke from Saville Row,
he risks no creases, stiff backed in the car,
a black Buick finning Commercial Road.
He looks as though his thoughts don't parallel
with rationale. He wants to be a star.

His scheming's binary. Ronnie's psycho
and needs editing—he's an elephant
his creased chin swinging like a trunk.
Their hit list escalates like rising shares.
Each move they make commissions an Oscar.
They ripped up the Watney Street gang blind drunk.

He dreams of federating criminals
to family and going underground—
a restaurant and shooting gallery
part of headquarters and Diana Dors
coming on late night squeezed into a gown
bumping her nipples out like petit fours.

His marriage shatters. Men make gangsters wives:
women are breakably disposable.
His wife ran out into the clubby night
when Ronnie broke a leg off the table
and had a go. She ended up that scared
she killed herself—pills all over the bed.

He needs to kill and do it ritually
to match his size with Ronnie's: skin for skin.
They're homicidal buddies, but he's scared:
Ronnie goes further and there's no appeal
in a face shiny as a boxing glove.
He knows the art is learning not to feel.

A contract's out on Jack the Hat. He drinks
himself into slow burn irrational rage
and knows he'll do it to avenge his wife
of insults. Ronnie's got a walk on part
as spectator. They set Jack up and steam.
He has it all rehearsed, but knows it's life.

Exit Marilyn Monroe

Blue fog browses on Fifth Helena Drive
in smoky opalescent swirls.
She targets her headache with Demerols.
The room's a mess.
She fits into a size too small
green Pucci dress

and feels the panic come alive
like radio inside her head.
It's Jack and Bobby Kennedy
who want her out. She fucked Jack in the bath
big as a steamy limo with gold taps
and now he wants her dead.

She won't let her red diaries go;
the ones that have the Cuba leak.
Custodial Bobby beat her up
so hard it took an osteopath
to get her back on set. His anger
blanks her like a psychopath.

Her hair's so blonde, she plays with it
like indoors sunlight come to fit
the throbbing contents of her brain.
She's happiest working on green
surprises planted out—fritillaries
and how it's come again a bean

trailing exuberant red flowers.
Deadheading's like an end to all:
the studios, a put on face,
counting the calories. She'd like to go
to the moon or Mexico.
Two snoops keep ringing on her bell.

Bobby's expected, or he's due,
diffident with affluent cool.
His business deals would fill a swimming pool
with dollars; but he won't come true.
He cheats like Jack. She storms her hair.
His shirts are blue Brooks Brothers blue.

She stands outside. The CIA
watch her watching them in a black Packard.
She shields her eyes against the sun,
turns round and Bobby's standing there.
He shouts before he slaps her flat
and very hard.

She locks the door, but he'll be back.
Her facial bruise matches the one
like a blue Asia on her ribs.
Her sleepers look like granular gym weights
stacked in a sealed amber bottle.
Cramming the lot's like swallowing a gun

composed of bitter paste.
She can't think clear. The car's outside.
Her sunflowers brim like yellow dinner plates.
They'll get her before she can suicide.
She looks out. Bobby's in his blue shirt sleeves
standing motionless at the gates.

Gay News

Tucked in a Kensington kiosk
you had to ask
for Dennis Lemon's inspirational
legit above ground headliners
bringing the subterranean out

of the criminalised ghetto:
GAY NEWS in bold black capitals
firm like the first knuckle of rain
accelerating to a thunder shower.
The numbers grew. Two syllables

lucked out like a covert mantra
bringing a sense of family
to being fugitive and queer.
Word shimmied through the Earls Court blocks
as though a top note started low

now stood out very clear.
The disparate took up the cause,
friend meeting friend and counted in
amongst the city's dispossessed,
but identified as outlaws.

Dennis as the progenitor
to wrapping an arm round the lost
threw it over London's rooftops,
brought in the lonely, East and West,
squeezed a firm torso North and South,

the sunlight sitting on his desk
like gold hairs foresting an arm.
The news took off. The gossip too.
A pretty boy like a putti
posed centre-spread in pink not blue,

his defined body muscular.
Lib started in the undertow
the way a hidden river flows
beneath a city, force concealed,
but present in the current's beat

each time it surfaces and runs
as a reminder, it's still there.
The editorial had it spot on,
measured the moment, the first Pride
spilling pink banners on the air.

1965
BEAUTIFUL LOSERS

Beautiful Losers

The skinny writer sits facing the sea,
terraced on Hydra, pre-fame, pre-Songs Of,
pre-Songs From A Room, 116 lbs of turned-down mood,
salty red geraniums in a pot,
a gravely Ray Charles record blued in its grooves,
The Genius Sings The Blues as accompaniment
to speed-fuelled writing sixteen hours a day,
the sunset flaring on his retina
like a red yoke splayed in the pan
to detonate in crackle. He works lines
like someone hotfooting a mountain trail
up past nomadic goats, friable dust,
to vision chaptered on a height
where clouds space over like spun candyfloss.

Beautiful Losers. We're all walk-on parts
inside his fiction. He works in its grip
like someone brushing off a python's scales,
but still eluding strangulation.
His neural wreckage floats around his brain like space-junk,
the breakdown rising on him from amphetamine
and affective disorder.
The sea deposits bleached myths on the sand,
starfish, stripped fish-spines, a statue's bronze ear,
cuttlefish bones
shaped like a girl's Size 3 shoe, a mashed orange crate.
Someone wades out of the surf, freeze-framed in 1965,
glazed in a black tie-side bikini.
He hallucinates her as Catherine Tekakwitha,
his Mohawk protagonist, metamorphic saint,
the woman stepping out
of words, like a salmon nosing through spray.
He's burnt by over-reach, the novel in him like nuclear fission.
He'll stay up all night, lay work down like a road
shaped for the future, for successive decades of readers
in a post-dated universe, go in,
pick chords on a guitar, and feel his head
throb in the darkness like it might explode.

Sky High 1965

The rent boy outside Piccadilly Boots
suns like a lizard on his patch,
his eau-de-nil cashmere V-neck

gifted by Jeremy Thorpe.
The sunlight's travelled in so far
it's jet-lagged on arrival.

In Kensington Anna Kavan's
reworking Ice: Burroughs shoots speed
into the novel's aorta.

In Shepperton J.G. Ballard's
tuned to a visionary ray,
neural as the Mods in Ham's Yard

pill-heading alternative states.
Jeremy Thorpe's at Westminster
thinking of Alex in his green jumper—

a soft exterior to rough trade.
Go East to Whitechapel, the Krays
are warming guns, like a good wine

coaxed to room temperature.
Crime builds like Beethoven's 9th in their heads.
Their suits are sharper than James Cagney's.

Andrew Oldham's zonked on a beach
in Miami. The sea rolls war
from Vietnam into its pebbled speech.

Jeremy Thorpe un-masts a spotty tie.
Back on his Dilly circuit he looks up
into a blue sky, miles high.

Burn

Keith's slept-in hair's their signature
a profile like Cro-Magnon crow
picking chords on a ruined hotel bed.

They're roomed up at the City Motor Lodge,
the all-American clouds breeze over
like Wall Street data on a thermal high.

Bottled by an antagonist
Brian's skull lesion's like the Grand Canyon
boiling with paranoia.

Keith's been electrocuted, chainsaw buzzed
at Sacramento, bolted flat,
laid out on stage, his hush puppies

doing their insulating trick.
Mick wears white Capezio ballet shoes
to androgenise sophomores.

Charlie's like a bespoke Taoist,
a savant whose brushes dictate
circadian rhythm to the beat.

Bill's bass licks play descending stairs,
the way down always the way up.
He builds a wall into their melody.

They've shed R&B and soul skins
for folk rock armour, upped their clout
as meanies with an attitude.

They craft their future in four days
compressed studio time, tool their best
and instantaneous Aftermath

at RCA, flaked out behind locked doors
with Brian dubbing harpsichord
that gentle it's like manicure.

She's Not There—The Zombies

A middle England tweak at loss,
a chamber music madrigal
garlic-spiked with R&B;

the singer's quavery vibrato thins
like jet vapour in the sky
airbrushed out one summer's day

scored with burn-hole memories:
poppies rashing grizzled furze
as consorts to frilled scabious?

Ubiquitously plaintive
the song takes room in everyone
opening up scar-tissue round

a wound that begs reminder
or glowers with a red-alert
that won't permit erasure.

The vulnerability's the thing,
a simmery naivety
that's plaintively elegiac,

helplessness investing a tone
underscored by disbelief
at her going, at her gone.

It's the way hurt's polarised
to little things, gets captured here,
the sassy colouring of her hair,

a walk that's unrepeatable,
all matched by the incredulous
astonishment, she won't be back

and nothing of her signature
survives, except the emptiness
crowding the moment with her scent.

Eric Burdon

Truculently smashed
his shot voice leathering gospel
like he's aiming bar-room punches;
he's ursine, grizzly, brain fade,
a New Orleans prodigy
on autopilot self-destruct,

disintegrating in the act.
He builds 'House of the Rising Sun'
with raucous empathy,
puts up a Northern scaffolding
around its structure, partners death
by burning in the ruin.

His invidious manager's
ex-military, an SS smile like wire:
and tries with drug coshes
to work a frequency,
squaddying spin into the nerves,
taking the fat cat's scoop of loot.

Hits come and go like ball lightning,
leaving a sticky residue
of burnt sugar.
He's baptised in bourbon, rye,
a diver butting a full vat
headfirst.

The road's exciting; it demands
the best of him, when legless.
He's stretched across America,
his bones ground into the highway,
brains scrambled in each hotel room,
50/50 psychotic.

He chills some days, rooms with Hendrix
even his time out's epic.
The wind drops. He sits on its tail
and fingerprints the sun.
He's white, he's black, he's blue, he's red:
the catastrophic war drags on.

Marianne Faithfull

The King's Road gamine iconised
by rock bon vivants, zipping it
in a shimmied Mustang Sally.

Chelsea's a cornucopia
of frothy boutiques: she'll load up
at Granny Takes a Trip

or riffle Biba's simmery
fantasia for plum velvets,
a crochet mini-skirt.

A demi-monde chanteuse, her songs
are fragile, flock-wallpaper things,
no hint yet of their tortured grab.

Spliffy bohemianism rules
the quality; at Courtfield Road
Brian Jones is a petit-four

placed on a cerise cushion.
The elect drive Rolls', invest
in serendipitous antiques.

She's Jagger's blousy rock chick
fêted, thrown into the air
like customised confetti.

The drugs are Smarties with a kick,
they make her see her own TV
as substance commentary.

The party lasts for a decade,
the guests get reinvented, die,
or stare at the King's Road transformed

by update, like a corridor,
revamped, redecorated, framed
for a new cortège to pass through.

Good Vibrations

A choral shimmer, sparkly vibe,
their vocal rondure's summery
cresting on layered harmonies,
an aspirant, etherealised
busily up-there pop mantra

to a sun, sex and surf ideal,
a beachy, druggy absolute,
a light-fantastic energy
synthesised in buzzy cells.
Their double-tracked incantatory

scripted litanies to hip youth
are polished with bright airiness
and ripple with sleigh bells, wind chimes,
harpsichord, flutes and theremin
and open like a flower to the light

a morning glory's thrilling blue.
Brian's the vibey panjandrum
directing studio-castrati
who pray before they fine-tune words
to a bleached-out transparency.

LA's the new Jerusalem
to the appointed surf-city
cognoscenti: Aldous Huxley
his attic stocked with LSD
acting as prescient guru

to mind-spacey collegiates,
flower-children, love-in advocates,
folk-rootsy nomads, pacifists,
pot-smoking sutra-reading heads,
desert fathers on chopper bikes

a revisioned community
struck up like sunflowers on the coast
all inclined heliocentrically
to the pouring source, air-waved pop,
the Beach Boys' tuneful liturgies.

The wave runs and they ride it fast
with repeat hits all coloured by
a tremulous Pacific blue
their lives turned over in the swash
littering its crash casualties.

They hold up. Brian churns to fat
and solitary artistry.
The music hangs in, circulates
as metabolised 1960s
speakered from a Deuce Coupe and heard

along the coast as a themed chant
to something ultimately visionary,
a love invasive as the sea
at Huntingdon and universalised
by youth as melodic descant.

The Last Time

The LA sunshine's coded 1965,
arrived at 736,000 miles per second
to polish a hotel window
with a pink and green rainbow
tracking a rhomboid on a late sleeper

surfacing in a mashed and clothes-spilled bed,
guitar cases stashed on the floor,
the blonde beside him sitting up
checking the autograph on her left arm
and in a peach-flush shimmying for the shower...

Later, the band convene at RCA,
a cleaner sweeps the studio's parquet floor,
they have all three, A, B and C,
high white ceilings and live echo chambers,
gobos for spectators, metal doors,

Neumann and Telefunken microphones,
a Neve console, ALO's hunch
building the audio layers with guitars
on a loping, hypnotic 'The Last Time',
punchy with its contagious hook...

Phil Spector livewires in to hear the sound,
maroon suit, mirrored Chelsea boots,
he wants to face it volume up,
tunnel clean through the sonic corridor
and pitch himself at its monitored core...

He stays behind, plays bass on 'Play With Fire,'
the morning sun blasting tomato red
over a 4am Sunset Boulevard,
the studio cleaner got into the mix,
brushing in corners, echo on each sweep.

Brian's off the Wall

Another desultory three-star hotel,
Britain reviewed from limos, Bradford seen
from the hard shoulder of the motorway…

Their haul's provincial. Brian's airline bag
contains the evidence, his whiskey pact
feeding a malt to his dependent's need—

a bottle a day gone AWOL
replenished with chunky Scottish-clan brands,
the empties body-bagged like casualties…

It's pressure in his nerves blows fuses out,
his epileptic blackouts, seizures, fits,
his panic arriving with the choked roar

of a tube's build-up and braked counter thrust.
Each day the same reckless fan-crazed assault,
ripped jacket, violated shirt and hair,

marauding offensives, a twisted fist
aimed for the jaw, a rocky get away,
the car jostled by an opposing wall

of mini-skirted hysterics, teenies
mad on the image and 'Not Fade Away'.
Brian's the capricious all-hours drinker,

the bibulous sophisticat left out
of band meetings, the solitary deposed
leader turned nervy, disinherited

of a rock-kingdom, as they slide through wet
towards another cut short date, the night
building behind them as blue swaggy cloud.

Play with Fire

Take a blues man and he colours
choked gospel deep South
as though a carp turned over

in refracted depths
flush in a pond
cool fire bleeding orange...

Elmore James, Chuck Berry,
Bo Diddley, Willie Dixon,
plaintively grainy numbers

slouch-voiced, drawlish raw,
each lament protested
from a subterranean cellar.

Blues cracks the voice
like lived-in leather
roughed out Muddy Waters

and insolent Jagger
sparking up Negroid
on Little Red Rooster

hanging out the notes
like offensives on a line
then licking them with breath

and punchy harmonica
arrogant the white boy way
of giving blues a sex change.

Aftermath

1

On Mother's Little Helper, Jagger's sneer
denouncing age is counterpoint
to fine wrinkles drawn from a sitar.

2

Stupid Girl's uncurtailed misogyny,
the singer means it with his venomous
jabby vocal authority.

3

Brian's twinkly dulcimer on Lady Jane
works through the song texture like a red carp
nudging a still pond after rain.

4

Marimbas as the subtext to she's dumb,
the lippy thermal the real dominant
in pressing home Under My Thumb.

5

The slide guitar's so dreamy it's film-scored
into a tetchy Doncha Bother Me,
the singer acting petulantly bored.

6

A bluesy, wailing, foghorned signature,
the harmonica's phrase on Goin' Home
sounds like it's squeezed out of the underworld.

7

Flight 505 punches imperatives
out of a crisp ensemble—departure gates
jumpy like bees around a hive.

8

A tight-lipped reappraisal, High And Dry
plays out a breezy emotional tide-mark;
a rock pool bottled with blue sky.

9

She's lost her moment, like a stiletto,
the obsolete girl on Out Of Time
chipped off like red gloss on a toe.

10

The sweet and sharp of youthful loneliness
wrung into It's Not Easy permeate
the song like scent a flimsy dress.

11

The perfect stranger sits in every bar,
a plaintive I Am Waiting mirrors change
like a face sighted from a speeding car.

12

Jagger's the polished apple and the core,
Take It Or Leave It has dismissive threat
to someone crawling back for more.

13

Think's a résumé, the sub-aqueous sax
recalling hard times bettered, moving on,
but keeping blues roots in the mix.

14

Equivocations: What To Do spells gain
to the protagonist: he'll think her back
for reappraisal in the London rain.

Sun Going Down (on me)

Mid-decade's the high water mark—
the Stones in 1965
washed by angry undertow,
a tentacular feeler
twitching an adhesive lasso

round Brian's jugular,
dragging on a manager
whose liner notes are proto-punk
Clockwork Orange cocktailed
with up yours yahoo.

They've scrapped 'Could You Walk On Water?'
for its messianic archetype.
Lennon crossed the Mersey
the salt on his toes
a filigree stigmata?

Jagger drops in at the Chelsea
in a black and white check suit.
Dylan's too stoned to look up,
contemplating a fragment
written on his boot.

The day comes up everywhere,
only the sun's oranger,
the summer bluer at Southend,
Brighton and Honolulu.
The dead are counted in the air.

Oldham's clinging to a cork
skating in the deep end,
his bipolar disorder
disrupts his chemistry and peaks
like a mid-air disaster...

Brian's dodgy, hatching plots,
legless, slurry, out of it.
The sixties shift like changing chords,
a figure held and lost again
like sunshine after early morning rain.

MODS AND CELEBRITIES

Pete Meaden—In Memoriam

The unacknowledged leader of the pack,
Pete Meaden weirding it down Monmouth Street,
a blue, red and white target on his back

in circa rainy 1963.
The Mod progenitor, his suss is cool,
he does most projects telepathically.

His band the High Numbers are now the Who,
blueprinted by his image-strategy.
He's sold out to Kit Lambert. Nothing's new.

His attitude spells ambiguity,
King Mod who's made a cult of purple hearts
to screen his vulnerability,

has shatter-lines inside his nerves.
He thinks round corners, mostly laterally.
He wears Bilgorri jackets with tight sleeves.

Things happen. There's no knowing why.
He got the message: new look, new decade,
by staring at a white wide-angled sky.

Others have dipped into his chemistry,
a boutique opens, ostentatious, camp,
a fashion changes between two and three...

The kids sniff out an alley off Beak Street,
John Stephens' frilly emporia:
his colours generate a livid heat.

Their prototype's off somewhere, like the Scene,
his brain already fired: when he sees blue,
its components split to yellow and green.

He moves too fast, and speed has blown his mind,
he's messed up, driving his thoughts like a car
clean through the present, with no past behind.

Mods

An edgy, narcissistic cult,
a group assembled in Ham Yard,
sharp-suited, clothes obsessed
to minutiae of button shapes:
Soho's their patch, when blocked on pills
purple hearts, a.k.a. Drynamil,
SKF granules engineered
for cool, speedy euphoria.
Carnaby Street aficionados
in striped blazers, knife-seamed hipsters,
candy-coloured button-downs,
hair fixed by invisible lacquer,
they're a scooter hegemony,
teenage fashion sophisticates,
clubby, tight-knit misogynists,
neat, cute and immaculate.
They burn to live and live to burn
on optimal R&B;
their bands detonating the floor
with punky energy,
the snappy Small Faces and the Who
at the Lyceum and Marquee.
They're style elitists, up all night
at the Flamingo, out at dawn
pirating market-stalls for thrift
a box jacket or snakeskin boots,
mirrors for a Lambretta stack,
obsessive in their serendipity,
fading the moment, high on it,
flooring the kickstand, horneting
a silver bike to Stamford Hill.
Their youthful coup's all self-destruct,
an auto-combustive signal
to blaze brightly for a few years
jacketed in a union jack,
and take no prisoners, least of all themselves,
but disappear, as though the lot
took off, and migrated into the night,
and kept on, without thought of turning back.

The Marquee

Soho's rogue cell, a cavernous
fire-power arena, Mod pundits
excerpting style from sussy leaks

carried downwind like pollen.
They're narcissistic, dance alone
to the cool image of themselves

as a sexless cognoscenti,
married to French blues, black bombers,
blocked on amphetamine.

The club's the buzz-word like the Who
raking it with Stratocasters,
revving a jeep through burning amps.

The girls double, orbit themselves,
outriders to a hegemony
bonded by sharp seams, knife-edge vents.

Tonight it's The Creation scrape
Les Paul strings with violin bows,
their free form feedback menacing

a blues song with collagist pop.
They're attitude dressed up to kill,
like plugged-in situationists.

They action-paint their finale,
set fire to it, as though a hive
released a squall of irate bees.

Later, they spill to into Wardour Street,
club-hoppers with their glassy trick
of detached politesse,

a Mod cult joy-riding scooters
through the West End, burning rubber
as tattoos on the rainy streets.

Mods vs Rockers

Lambrettas fleeted by the Palace Pier,
so gizmo-stacked with spotlights, mirrors, furs,
they're fetish artefacts or weaponry,

a scooter conclave flying Union Jacks,
their owners posed in parkas, crew-necks, boots,
beside a lazily collapsing sea,

a green-grey tide that's clouded eau-de-nil.
Their opponents are leather-cased and mob
in jabby echelons, still holding back

from confrontation. Someone throws a stone
and scores a hit, as signal to attack
the modish poseurs in their fashion kit,

who now assemble, as an irate pack,
stones sorted in their fists, all industry
and swarming at a run across the beach.

Volley and counter-volley form a rain
of whizzing pebbles; the groups separate,
as though deliberating strategy.

Crowds mass the promenade, the boys in blue
wade into skirmishes: a tanker scrolls
its orange hull across the skyline's sill...

A fist salute, and now the sides engage
in running combat, skeins of skinny Mods
busy with sticks, force their antagonists

into a routed, heads-down, licked retreat,
the biker boys stampeding for shelter,
bottles and stones missiled around their feet...

The day is won: the Mods raise a salute
to their ideal, then scooter off pursued
by thuggish police vans through the Brighton Lanes.

Small Faces

Wapping's river children
upgraded on the current
the 1960s happening
in the city's neural mix,
from Ham Yard to the Marquee
as Mod progenitors
they tune into the archetype—
white jeans and candy-striped blazer,
check button-downs, Drynamil,
a silver chromed Vespa...
Their diminutive leader's
effervescently loquacious
stacked up on boot heels
like his bluesy Delta voice,
a cockney Aretha Franklin
turning a song over
like bringing down a lion.
We programme in 'Tin Soldier'
for its rippy vocal tool
a pop edge stab at gospel,
the singer dead by fire,
gone the way his voice shook
flame into the words,
set the lyric burning
then turned his back,
watched the river finned with mist
a generation die,
a red chemical sunset
elegise the sky.

The Dealer

Lean, and headed Sherwood Street—
B-side of Piccadilly's node,
his fuchsia-tinted glasses screen
London's grey Rothko monochrome,
its subtext rain and rainier
presentiments in June.
His hooky
Dylanesque terminology
has overdosed on Blonde on Blonde,
his rose-flecked floral shirt's labelled Lord John.
He's anonymity: the man
inside and out The Man
who never stays, and deals
by sleight of hand.
Acid, speed and DMT,
no bad cuts, are his currency,
insidiously moving through
the crowds as a virtual body,
a post human fade-out, a bleached
discontinuous identity.
Jamie's his contact; a speed freak
band entrepreneur, stylish Mod
clubber at the Marquee,
who's never late, his money clean
inside an envelope.
He sees him windowed in the same café.
The H users space outside Boots.
Avoid. Avoid. His stash is sealed
inside an album's cardboard sleeve—
the unsuspicious gift he'll make
to Jamie of the Small Faces'
Odgen's Nut Gone Flake.

The Who

Soho's the Mod epicentre,
the Marquee 1968,
Townshend's abusive Fender smashed
into stacked amps, the flaming neck
trashed to debris like Concorde's overshoot

grilled to a flash on take off.
They kamikaze 'Substitute',
decapitate the mike, Daltrey
poling the stand through the drum-kit,
giving it all on a cyclonic bash

at a compressed, blow every fuse
lobotomised 'My Generation'.
The song deconstructs round its core
like sonic fall out, the band nailed
to rhythm like they're tube surfing.

They're hyped-up pyromaniacs
littering hits through a smoke-wall,
power-pointing 'I Can't Explain'
with impromptu ante -
the feedback a quarrelsome roar.

Kit Lambert watches from the stage,
lugubrious as Kit Marlowe,
entrepreneurial manager
trawling the night in a black car,
alleying same-sex assignations.

They nuke each number, shoot it down,
annihilate its simplistic
play-ravaged Top Ten associations,
exit as brawlers, the drummer
striking the singer like a rattlesnake.

Twiggy

An Indian rope trick
of anatomy
Neasden's Lesley Hornby
a.k.a. Twiggy
recreating bedroom wall good looks
thin as a Giacometti.
She walks into 1966
sexless in a ribbed polo shirt
and crochet mini
a gangster's teeny moll,
a gamine, eyes that caterpillar lashed
they're dark as rain
on violets, jet saucers
that are third sex, Martian
or peculiar
to a suburban extraterrestrial.
She's unrehearsed as a white page
demanding ink,
ingenuous in the role
of making it up as she goes,
naivety finding its winning point
in creating the part
that wrong, it's right.
Twiggy goes global on glossies—
her thinness making aliens
in violet boots desirable,
flat as sexy.
Her aesthetic's being so ordinary
she's always out of context in a shoot
her diminutive Chinese feet
so small they're bandaged?
She's the untutored celeb
a cherry stuck to her nose,
amused, quizzical and surprised
as though caught looking through a window
on the tips of her toes.

Terence Stamp and Michael Caine

Stamp and Caine—bright young things
at the Terrazza Trattoria
too masculine to be an item?
Both bespoke stylists dressed by Doug Hayward
as classic un-Mod modern,
both flash with provocative imposture.

Stamp turns his body motorway busy
doing Royal Canadian Air Force work outs.
His good looks have a cockney imprimatur,
a roughed-out imperfection won
from upgrading his genes into
the face of 1964; but hard

as though they're a try-on for fame
and have no staying power.
Caine skews in from the April shower,
his white Burberry turned patchy from rain
like a discoloured wall. His blue eyes freeze
surroundings like a mortuary.

They're branded queers living on Ebury Street.
The London rain's like diamonds when you're up
and dedicated tedium when down.
Stamp's a blonde big part Billy Budd,
a movie star chasing the shortest skirts.
Caine's older and sensitive to put down.

Even married Stamp cohabits with Caine.
The black bathroom's bottled with luxuries—
Habit Rouge, Dior and Vetiver;
the pink soap tablet's like scented money
rewarding big male hands.
Stamp's like the burnt toast. Shrimpton the honey.

They fall apart: a rumbling family
fault lines accelerating in the grid.
They split one day of bright effusive rain,
Stamp's suitcases loaded by the cabby,
Caine indoors tightening his fist
knowing he'll walk on set and blow his lid.

Colour

Colour goes up-tempo, the beat
of primaries and secondaries
mixed like a salad:
Peter Blake, Allen Jones, Hockney
pointing up tones in how we see
1961-64
as blues—Hockney's worked-out blonde nudes
claim blue as an accessory
to being gay—the shower or swimming pool
a very modern way
of emphasis; the skin
desirably the colour of LA.
Or take a Richard Hamilton
interior, the carpet's lime-green block
a shock
like urban jungle on the floor,
a green imagined green, its bite
so tonic it's like excitement
at finding out the city's heart's
acacia green not rainy grey.
Badges on blue—when Blake goes pop
a generation hits the street
as bright young things dressed like his art
in colours that explode.
Hodgkin reaches the apogee
of tropicals—his blues, yellows and pinks
creating hotter ecospheres
that show
in Mrs Nicholas Monro's
facial confection: an abstract zebra
slashed with pink and blue handlebars.
60s' colour's like a heart-shaped helium balloon
nosing the ceiling in a loft,
the expectation vertical—
the way up bright orange and green
the climb down pastels
pistachio ice cream soft.

The Book of the Post-Mods

A gang tag's demographic signature
licks along Soho's Marshall Street
signed off with a lemon ISBN

7-149924-92-1
the book of the post-Mods avenging cult
injected into street iconography

as a citric insignia.
Vented jackets, Ben Sherman button-downs,
unreconstructed all-male cool

given a pristine makeover,
they're alumni of the first London wave
attitudinising Ham's Yard

in a white hipster 1962.
The reassembled do style on their patch,
bottled in a Soho alley,

videophones gunned in their hands and neat
with smart facts about polymers
in scratch-resistant car paint—a Coupe's

coating with a ceramic base
the molecules strongly cross-linked.
The deep Med-blue gloss on a Jaguar.

They hack US Air Force reports
of weapons systems stored in space,
and klatchily convene around Beak Street,

as though trapped in a disruptive space-time.
They're pointed both forward and back—
silver Vespas gone like Steve Marriott

into history's solvent—the new
filled with their presence on a Saturday
tricked out with blue sunlit sky winning through.

Sherry's

What if you could: retrieve it again, lost time?
The 60s impossible to touch
as yesterday's sunlight and its splash

like a yellow tabby sitting on the stairs,
its epitaph a red Fender
auctioned into history,

£200,000 for a Hendrix axe
stolen at Primrose Hill, the thief pursued
in gutsy flurries to the underground,

then dematerialising in the blobby crowd.
On Portobello Road the clues are there
like DNA, a decade's residue

retrieved as flashbacks. A girl tubed in boots
drives a red E-type Jaguar
directly out of 1968

towards a pink blossom whipped Powys Square?
She hasn't aged: her Biba carriers
are chunky as a Size 10 pharaoh's hoard.

Carnaby Street's demagnetised,
brooded over by Shakespeare's boozy head,
but browse the corridor that's Ganton Street

and Sherry's Mod renaissance shop
brims with authentic 60s styles
cut from originals, floral paisleys,

pearl-sized white polka dots on navy blue
button downs, John Smedley jumpers
in ice cream colours, take your pick

and recreate the fitted masterpiece
a shirt becomes worn Mod, the collar's roll
shaped like an ear, the point dangerously sharp.

SHOPPING

Carnaby Street

Labyrinthed in Soho's grid—
near Kingly, Beak and Marshall Street,
John Stephen's alleyed centrepiece,
outré, dandified and camp,
is like a dress rehearsal romp,

a maverick's retake on style
from macaronic Regency,
to pink hipsters, paisley shirts,
six button back vented DB jackets
an edgy detail to their cut.

From a backroom in Beak Street
this visionary shaped the line
of a renaissance, the hot spill
of zany colours propositioning
the rebellious and the cool.

Grape curls and rebel Jimmy Dean
constrained hubris, he's all mystique
and introspection, shielded eyes
and private life locked up in a walnut,
he's that elusively shut.

The street takes off, cross-fertilised
by a gay and Mod clientele—
the fussy and trimly austere,
then blows into the paradigm
of an explosive youth zeitgeist—

a cult Mecca in which to shop
for lambs wool crew-necks, floral shirts,
cavalier red crushed velvet suits,
candy-striped watch straps, hounds-tooth slacks,
all exaggeratedly OTT.

He steps out of a silver Rolls
companioned by a shepherd dog
fluffy as a white powder puff:
his work ethic—100 hours a week,
tutoring each collection stitch by stitch.

He's king of cloth on Soho's patch—
pop stars riffling through every rail,
the detonation impacting
for a decade, he looking up
surprised, before striking a match.

Ossie Clark's Quorum

The blue jeans art school protégé
walks out of 1959
into hallucination.
His patterns are like new planets
sighted in the galaxy's bright doughnut

of dusty star clusters.
A lid's lifted off the World's End—
Chelsea opens like a sunflower's
heliocentric radar.
His skirts go micro-micro

slashes of violet crêpe, taupe silk,
his snakeskin jackets are ophidian
leechings of cobra and python.
He cuts to shock
an individuated youth

with satin, purple velvet coats,
a Restoration ruff
on Carolinian shirts.
The King's Road pours like a river
directed to his door,

a current working to oppose
repression, machismo, war,
the old world with its killing fields
and colour-coded gender
challenged for its toxic scars,

its militant agenda.
His clothes ripple like tropical
fish off the Bahamas—
they're sensual to the fingertips,
slippery like an oyster....

Ossie's couture king in SW3,
a maverick without a crown,
scissors in hand, a droopy joint
sighting his work—his labels out
like coloured rain all over town.

Shopping

A crocodile of Hendrix
lookalikes, fuzzed Afros
cascading on military braid—
that one's Napoleon
flash-forwarded from Waterloo

to Covent Garden
1969.
He's en route to Indica
eating a Ricotta pancake
with purple broccoli and pancetta...

He's parked his gold Mini Cooper
somewhere back of the Opera House.
A confection of city clouds
seem to conceal the bigger change
happening at vanishing point,

like John Lennon's up in the sky
looking down with an orange eye
on London's navel.
From a window on Long Acre
someone's playing Disraeli Gears—

the panning sounds like thunder
bottled in an underpass.
Clapton's ruminative figures
shifting furniture mid-brain
with tweaky wah-wah.

September in the city
smells like Lapsang Souchong.
Shelley's on Old Compton Street
reading Aeschylus
to a funky beat...

Shopping's like building pyramids
that instantly dematerialise.
He cuts it through the crowd, the sun
behind him, every step alert
to the new ethos won.

The Blue Danube

A gossipy Mod locus—
the 60s are decided there,
what's in, what's out, the thermal hot
on dress statements that last a day
from Friday night

to frothy Saturday.
Chelsea outside, the Who are buzz,
skinned in white jeans and Union jacks;
the Mods started in Walthamstow,
migrated West, a crosstown fire

of attitudes and Lambrettas
territorialising Soho,
then wedging South and West again
scattershot across the King's Road
as French jumper invaders

epitomising cool.
Today the gossips Jagger/Jones
as a sexual item:
it all went wrong, Mick's red lipstick
signposted on the bathroom—

B's a faggy little bitch
heading for oblivion..
The word is out and chewed like gum
to an exhausted flavour.
The gay club basemented downstairs

hangs on to the rumour
like biting a lip.
Sensation's hip.
They work on it, like throttling roar
to blue vapour.

Quentin Crisp fins through the crowds,
conspicuous for make-up.
The beat goes on. They search the charts.
The Small Faces are riding high
to do the cause a favour.

Swinging London

Two gay boys slip out of a Soho loo.
The law still squeezes like a python's grip.
They speak palare: one has a tattoo

dangerously visible to the decoy
hanging out underground all afternoon.
He's butchly feminine. A pretty boy.

London's villages synergise the beat
as a collective groove—it's in the air—
the speed of light travels under the feet.

Hockney's in town, his aqua swim-in blue
changing forever how we see water.
His technicolour turquoise comes up true.

The changes happen fast, metabolised
irregularly, like a B complex
kicking in power when it's least realised.

Pink Floyd go ballistic at the UFO,
their stratospheric Stratocaster overkill
injecting mania into the light show.

The Waste Land's synchronised to catchy pop,
Eliot and Hendrix panned through one speaker.
Kit Marlowe waits at the 14 bus stop.

The rain is happier for being rain.
Poetry's in the undertow; the word
keeps reshaping itself for a refrain.

Harrods seems less a barracks. Biba's in.
The epoch burns off rudimentary fat.
Kafka's its archetype: mosquito-thin.

The gays boys separate at Broadwick Street,
resume their double lives, as thunder builds
like scaffolding around the solid heat.

Making a Name

Ossie Clark and Mr Fish
scissors impresarios
ruching crêpe for bright young things
high-flyers
or jet setters like Mick Jagger
wearing scarlet Mary Quant
eyeliner.
Robert Fraser's gallery
shows the decade's innovators
he's all Jeeves & Hawkes, Thresher and Glenny,
gay like the Etonian dandy
Jeremy Thorpe with his rough trade
fished for with a green silk tie
on the rack at Piccadilly.
Lyndsay Kemp heroes in Flowers,
mime that's so ethereally
underworld, it's like a rose
transformed into a fist.
John Calder and Peter Owen
publish cutting-edge:
Burroughs, Beckett, Bowles, Mishima,
showcased from independent logos
hacking it against the grain.
Warhol's got his arts-lab Factory
done out like a trampish backroom,
all his freaky cognoscenti
wearing pink halos.
Yves St Laurent injects couture
with a Tiepolo palette,
pinks and blues to die for, reds
peppered by apocalypse.
Christopher Gibbs, trophies antiques
for Brian Jones' London flats,
names are spelled out by the sunlight
bringing data to the age,
millennia of photon parcels
illuminating centre-stage.

Shirts

Take a through
from Argyle Square
to John Stephens'
Carnaby emporia
the shirty Mecca
West End back street
smoky sunlight-hazed
modern to pop
as designer shopping
all those paisley whorls
and English rose floral
motifs and polka dots
white snowed on blues
or red like little moons
pointilistically exact
foppish shirts with dandified bibs
and lace-frothy cuffs
or heavy satin blouses
in purple or oyster
taupe and vermilion
cavalierly dashy
splashing from a frock coat
like amazing tumbles
from a parrot tulip
frilling a corolla.
See the new youth imaged
by audacious collars
twirly with carriers
a hair-screened Mick Jagger
a bobbed Steve Marriott
a red leather waistcoated
Pretty Things—Phil May
all jostling the bustle
for sartorial stand out
fishing for a garment
to bend gender kinky
black cabbing back

with ostentatious shirts
in a light peculiar
to being alive
at a given moment in a decade
going on autumn 1965.

Carte Blanche

Pate, rijsttafel,
cannelloni, caviar,
blintzes, Lowenbrau,
matzoh ball
soup, zucchini,
tagliatelle, lobster
bisque, hay-coloured
Chablis's chic
bouquet, tomatoes
de treille muscatel,
bouillabaisse,
stuffed calamari
on linguine, tofu burgers
and quesadillas,
terrine of duck,
goats cheese tatin,
fried potatoes, steak
tartare, marjoram
and tarragon frissoned
grilled spring chicken,
escalopes of salmon,
rosemary braised lamb
jarret, caramelised
carrots, Savoy cabbage
roesti, spaghetti,
saddle of venison,
sauve St. Emilion,
peppery Bourgogne,
macaroons, raspberry
champagne coulis,
crystallized ginger,
cocaine rocks,
ubiquitous
hamburgers.

Elegy for a Polka Dot Shirt

Unreconstructed 60s
ostentation snowed on blue
labelled Jacques Fath, tailored fit,
fished from Retro on a simmery
cloud hung-over August day,
bought for pop connotations—
high collar with flouncy points,
cotton married to the skin.
Medium size:
       38 cm:
structured for a defined waist
sexless to the vanity
of ownership.
Affordable at £15,
the item begged me to retrieve
its showy staginess.
       Outside, airless haze,
WII backpacking crowds
random like footage spilled into
a documentary.

Later I tore a fragile seam
tracking towards left underarm,
the fissure sounding like hot oil
pronouncing itself in a pan.
The tear backtracked through history
to the anonymous wearer,
who bought sensation, sold it on
into a chain, the onion skin
thinning from use;
       the scar re-sewn,
but evident, a little glitch
caught in the fabric like a blues

lament,
the singer head-bowed on a stool,
cooking up trouble, while the club
tug at his vulnerability
and modulate applause from hot to cool.

1966
ON POETRY'S TRAIL

Joe Meek

Joe's a cottage graffito
gives good head, goes Oh
Oh Oh
a Teddy boy Jean-Paul Belmondo
hair greasy as an Elvis pompadour.

A fugitive in Holloway
playing footsy, Oh
Oh Oh
dearie that's a painted toe
red as a vine-tomato.

Has a bathroom studio
wires gummed together, Oh
Oh Oh
gets freak compression, space echo
like a cupboard tornado.

Lives from instinct and not know how
roughs a demo and Oh
Oh Oh
sings the chorus high falsetto
colours it red and indigo.

Stays an impresario
scores big hits, then Oh
Oh Oh
plays with shotguns, wins with ouija,
takes his pills with an espresso.

Picks a decoy up below
the pavement, and Oh
Oh Oh
gets arrested, mean-queen Joe
waiting to go down. Oh no.

Blasts his landlady from zero-
range, then shoots himself, Oh
Oh Oh
Joe looks in and out the window
exiting in loud staccato.

The Hollies

Breezy up-mood harmonies
they shift from plateaus to a high
as through the song graduated
from Mancunian fog to instructive light.
Catch a rainbow in a glass
and have it swim, is how they sing
on 'Look Through Any Window':
their falsetto the rainbow's fin
as it shows purple.
They're pleasure-activists, their sound
that comfortable, it's like ripples
in watered silk; the plaintive catch
coming up rainy, 'Yes I Will',
put into corners by angular mood.
Clarke, Nash and Hicks, the choral three,
orchestrate urban surf, not blue
like the Beach Boys' Pacific themes,
but russety like autumn flowers,
spiky red dahlia and chrysanthemum,
their tone always affirmative
and pedigreed on 'I'm Alive'.
Just listen in, their moment seems
not frozen in a lost decade,
but expansive, as though climbing the stairs
in a high rise we met the sun
brimming orange on every floor
and heard a different song on each level,
a Hollies phrase accompany
the way up to the top.
They take you there by voice-ascent,
the aspirations small, but the ideal
perfectly executed, note by note
unrivalled as infectious pop.

Tim Hardin

His songs are gentle as roses
spilled in a foggy garden—
the dawn back of haze Beaujolais red.

Their melodies are grief-shaped chords,
fragile things for a bear-man
gone the way of morphine.

They have you think you missed the train
your love was on, and later sent
a cloud to follow as a poem.

The Walker Brothers

Take Wagner, Spector,
Big Bang production,
a three octave baritone
so feeling it registers
all loss as singular
and add percussion like a car
bouncing on its roof over
a cliff to a shattered swell
and that's a Walker signature
indexing sonic crescendo
to a loser's blue-streak theme,
a rainy-eyed persona
hunched on a street corner
with nowhere to go.
Take three eyebrow fringes
and 28 waist hipsters
dark shades and skinny suits
and moody postures
and a way with a ballad
like laying down a road
heroic and solid
in two minutes flat.
Take the lead singer's
inimitable gravitas
a voice constructing tone
from emotional thunder,
a presence cowed by stage fright
deep in his interior
phrasing his way out of impossible hurt,
that's Scott in his agonised
youthful appraisal of death
looking for an exit
before the lights go dead.
Take the food chain of hits
on a descending curve
the vocal rush spectacular
as a Land's End wave,

their epic formula sustained
three years before the crash,
their exit singing 'Walking In The Rain',
an apocalyptic pop finale
leaving a stormy sunset on the charts.

Over, Under, Sideways, Down—The Yardbirds

Beck's signature
circa psych mania
shapes a fuzzy collage
like sketching a nebula's
collapsed burn-out
round an orange core.

They're a sonic arts-lab
on 'Shape of Things',
feedback like a Jag's brakes,
or down there, melancholic,
Gregorian chant roofing
their sound like a forest.

The idea's Euclidean
giving shape to chaos,
pop experimentalists
dressing their songs
in an aural line,
fragmented, but perfect.

Asthmatic vocal,
the sneer's introspective:
'For Your Love's' so echoey
it comes out of a mall
or a blues cemetery
inside a tunnel.

Time's like a rogue cell
they make plastic on record:
'Happening Ten Years Ago'
is like cryogenics
the song laid down deep-freeze
for future resuscitation.

Too forward, they're zapped
by industry shenanigans,
their saucer-shaped music
weird like a sighting
coming back on itself
as a spacey parabola.

Dusty Springfield

The beehived panda's bouffant's faked,
a camp accessory, sassy
extension worn to fit the song.

Soul diva with a husky catch
in phrasing, her delivery
gives figurative shape to pain,

an R&B topology
to buried hurt, a gospel wail
heard like a night train prefacing

its entry to a tunnel.
She's all wedding-cake make-up,
broody mystique on spike heels.

Singing for her's like hiking up
the Himalayas, note by note
to dare the highest peak.

Diffidently angular,
she's a tortured sob sister,
a dykish artefact,

her problems diffused into drink.
She's torchy, and burns for lost love
in vocal embers.

Too complex, too ambivalent,
to join the sell-out rostra,
she's like the cherry on the rumbaba

the quintessential topping:
the stylist rolling notes that bruise
in stormy blues and purple.

Cecil Beaton photographs Jagger

The roué's white hat sips at lilac hair,
the effete aesthete, louche Sloaney
re-tops a glass of Veuve Clicquot Grande Dame

with spirally explosive molecules
tapering to a funnelled V,
like the inclusion of a zip.

He's Englished in the level heat,
cassis silk tie like blackcurrant
ribbed across vanilla ice cream.

He thumbs a misanthropic Graham Greene,
the plot bleached like the equator
revivified by Scotch and soda,

and feels the age-gap tighten like a belt
forced on the flight at 40,000 feet.
He's run flat up against déclassé love,

like Thomas Mann's for Tadzio,
the eunuch Jagger sequenced in his brain
as a repeat chemical high,

a tight-bunned hairpin-hipped androgyny.
His camera's their connecting eye,
the Nikon loaded for the shoot,

as though converting flesh to imagery's
the closest substitute for touch.
He's a style supremo, turned fidgety,

love in the air like ripe guava,
testosterone count risen in his groin,
pouting for the diffident star,

as though he's seventeen, not sixty-eight,
bored with The Quiet American,
and nervous, like he's waiting on a date.

Yoko Ono

Yoko's a Fluxus
classical pianist,
she rides a white cloud
like a dance-point pony
it's called inspiration,
and dips over summits,
Mount Fuji, St. Paul's
with its pumpkin-shaped dome
writing in diamond
Nov 6, 1966
a psychic gateway
open at Indica
like a white flower,
John in the centre
his neurons like anthers
taking in their meeting
under 'Ceiling Painting'
a canvas with a minuscule
word on it as a skylight.
White on white pieces,
some are transparent,
the chess set's a mirage
all smart molecules,
the one dab at colour
a Bramley's apple
cidery with autumn
grained in its skin,
positioned on Perspex
like a solitary planet.
He bites the explosive
fermenting juices,
takes a half moon out
chunked from the core.
Love's in the flavour
like a telepathic signal,
sweet, sharp and clear,
roundly salival,

the tree and the apple
got in one bite,
tasting of a Kent orchard
in damp russet sunlight.

Toe Polish

Two tango
brush and toe
slicked scarlet

Sandie Shaw's
dribbled blob
brushed locket—

shapes signal
a Mary Quant
chic logo

Ten wiggly toes
like minnows
up for text

glossed lacquery
as a Benedikt's mint
prized from green foil

Sandie's glaze
grosses scintilla
like bits in amber

fractal stuff
She's all pedic
scrutiny

tickly-tactile
flexing ten
jelly beans

vermilion tipped
blow-dried
to cool lava

Later nyloned
intaglios
she's barefoot

on Top of the Pops
crochet mini
netting skin

like hollow diamonds
patterning
white lozenges

teasingly
as she lip-syncs
dancey bubblegum

Paint it Black

Cooking like thunder
behind soufflé cumulus
the shock's the sitar's
elegiac attack,
a jangly Berber dissonance

of movable frets
colouring a signature
that's dejectedly black,
the motif so hooky
it jumps out like a pivotal

switch in direction
to a try-out decade,
the Stones turned funereal,
introspectively eclipsed,
seeing colour through brain fade

as ubiquitous black.
A chart-fêted ensemble
turned perverse with themselves,
nihilistic, reversionary,
squeezed the moment like an orange

of its Vit C elixir,
swung round on the King's Road
and saw the sun black.
Wind blew out of the summer
sparky with planetary glitter

inciting guitars
to register change.
Brian's jingly fingers
damaged in Tangier
no longer instructive

to baroque inflections,
closed down with Aftermath,
his tinkling recherché
prettified embellishments
sacrificed for raunchier hits.

On Poetry's Trail

It smells of freedom and it's peppery,
a wind blown out of nowhere—East to West,
transparent as a Hesse allegory,

the journeyer compelled to know himself
like the one plum tree kneeling in the lake.
Bob Dylan scratches at the interface

between lyric and basement prophecy,
his line so adept it creates the age
in colours of Californian poppies.

Dylan's the signifier in the dance,
his raw unconscious channelling alerts
a generation to his glottal drawl,

as he delivers an untutored line
big as America on which to build
a new, eventful, street-cred poetry.

Somewhere, the dreamer propped in a back yard
under a fig tree's dense, flippery shade,
jolts out of drifting free-float imagery

into a parallel reality
with Dylan's 'Subterranean Homesick Blues'
circulating from a top floor window

as spooky subtext to the hazy day.
He feels his trust attach itself to song
as a way forward, the tune's in his cells

and hanging on the air-waves everywhere.
The light inside the fig tree reads out time
by watching in on his activities.

Now he's connected, there's more dream around
immediacy, and figs are ripening
from deepest crimson to a purple rind.

Moroccan Interlude

A coyote wail
of power-chords over the casbah
howls from the Minzah's
immaculate tenth floor,
promises of Jajouka

entailed over kif
or majoun in a hookah,
Brion Gysin's caduceus
pointing up to the mountains
where Targuisti and Salah

confab with the tribe.
Brian's going ballistic
beating Anita
and bringing back Berbers
with tattoos on their vulvas...

Paul Bowles given entrée
noodles in for tea,
taciturn, saturnine,
in an ivory linen suit
he beats a fast retreat...

Cecil Beaton's fixated
by Mick's derrière
and how he angles a finger
smoking like Dietrich,
orchestrating a Stuyvesant

like a trout fisher
lobbying a fly.
Mick dances for his mincey
spectatorial sugar daddy's
royal demeanour,

a queeny voyeur
perfect as a calla
lily in a Ming vase,
wearing a Harrods green silk tie
in the desert heat.

Keith drives off with Anita
in his chauffeured Blue Lina,
the party gone cool,
like a jinn dumped pollutants
in the green swimming pool.

Brian's pilled up, hysterical,
left behind.
Beaton sniffs at a red rose
held like a powder puff
to his fine-boned nose.

Hotel Minzah

A coven at the Minzah
jajouka's understudy
delusionally schizoid—
twitchy Brian Jones
vamped in Berber jewellery
high on Elmore James
and all broken down

The whole Stones party
room-in to the music's
gutsy bluesy wail
Brian's asthma-panicked
weirded from occult
speak of death by water
and all broken down

Tangier smells of hashish
Paul Bowles as expat guru
lighting up a hookah
Brian's neurotoxic
sees his hands as flippers
sheeny as frog skin
and all broken down

All those Ossie Clark
gold brocaded coats
rupture at the seams
Mick's gone to the mountains
Brian's on the flat
plateaued in brooding
and all broken down

Paranormal quirks
keep on quizzing Brian
he's scared goose-pimplish
his killer's on his back
disguised as black on black
a hit man in an alley
and all broken down

Deserted and loaded
he'll watch his hands later
do violent shapes
like objects in water
Frazzled by the light
he'll lift up his shadow
and all broken down

Blood on his pigment
was the run-in murder
or domestic fracas?
No-one's in the foyer
if he's dead he's died
without a reminder
and all broken down

Dr Max

The limo fins across Park Avenue
2.30 am uptown—the city's brainstem
firing with nightlife, a Chevy
burning up parallel
shaped like a lipstick pink stealth bomber,

Brian back-seated in the black Lincoln,
hands on his chauffeur's shoulders—Frank
wearing a white cashmere roll neck
segueing into Lexington
ALO filmstarred in black shades

scanning the district's movie-set.
They park up. Buzz the entry-phone,
hit the click into reception,
breeze through Max's nocturnal waiting room
to a high ceilinged green office,

presidential photos framed on the wall—
Lyndon Johnson, JFK and Jackie,
suited bodyguards chinned at their shoulders
endorsing Max's special shots
of cocktailed vitamins and monkey glands

a.k.a. metamphetamine.
Jackie in a Halston pillarbox
stares star-struck from the broad oak desk.
Brian's the first to be shot up
to a speed-managed alert

a 48hrs optimal efficiency.
His shirt's a white chiffon gesture
worn like smoky fog.
Frank holds back. He won't do the drug.
Andrew's all compliant complicity...

Later downtown, they find Hendrix crashed out,
still plugged into the sound system,
flat on his back, guitar howling
in St Mark's Place, a strawberry dawn
coming up East Side like a thunderstorm.

A STONES DOSSIER

Acid King David

He's blend in along Maddox Street
an acid-freak entrepreneur,
selling paradisiacal VR
to foppish nouveau-riche pop stars
dressed in Cecil Gee mohair.

He's period in a floral shirt,
hair eyebrow-fringed and resolute
to tip his ears and shoulders.
His brain is microwaved by drugs:
he'll meet you on the corner.

Dealers are fictions. Dave's a wolf,
an ersatz Count, a legendary
messiah in a purple suit
doing his COEX chemicals
as psychoactive currency…

Dave's HQ is at Eaton Square,
Gibbs' antiques, a Jaguar
stoned in the space outside his door.
He squats on a gold eight-foot-tall
triangular chair raised above the floor

and disarranges a sitar.
Money comes easy. Rock gofers
handle it all undercover,
deliver bundles by chauffeur
in the rowdy Chelsea night.

Dave's suspect for the Redlands bust,
cleaning his skin by informing
on users with their incremental stash,
acid, speed, Moroccan hash,
mini-dispensaries bought on trust.

Dave's bad trip involves a black rat
a confrontational intruder
bigger than him, who stares him out,
tongue hoovering the polished floor,
pinning him there in a cold sweat.

He's up for nights: paints himself gold,
sits naked waiting for the sun
to feed him immortality.
The drug's his master: LSD
as visionary totality.

He'll split for California
when things get hot, do peyote
with desert groups, re-birth himself
in a hippie community
his new acid emporia.

Jumping Jack Flash

He's a hoodo mambo
strutting a rumba
white Africana
junglishly primal
his undertones glottaly
South London, Dartford.
Cool in a tiara
or mink balaclava
he's made up and trashy
to strut it on boards
like a bashy pasha
or Berber bellydancer
his undertones glottaly
South London, Dartford.
He's a symbiotic
Diaghilev, Nureyev,
finger-wagging exorcist
mean-eyed mesmerist
coming on vatic
his undertones glottaly
South London, Dartford.
He's uncontestably
freeze-framed 1960s
gender-antagonist
bitchy svengali
swatch-tongued and counting
his riches like Dali
his undertones glottaly
South London, Dartford.
He's a voodoo instructor
who won't let you in
a class infiltrator
a snappy alligator
in-concert contortionist
raunchily prurient
but with a limp wrist.
He's a bluesy avatar

runway infanta
a right to the roots star
rock epic exponent
his undertones glottaly
South London, Dartford

Keith Richards 1967

He's doped into unfazed passivity—
a blackout, roomed-up, quirky indolence,

a cool alert to inspirational riffs
that flicker through his foggy chemistry;

the way that 'Satisfaction' jumped from sleep
into a declamatory guitar phrase,

a buzzily infectious instant hook…
He's cooked by ennui, blanket lethargy,

this raffish squire in buskins moonishly
baffled by sunlight leaking through a blind.

He's prototypical 'go get a life
if you're not me,' his scissor legs stage style

an exercise in smart audacity—
a poppishly upgraded B.B. King.

He's schooled by ear, those days at Edith Grove
listening to vinyl wear in canyoned grooves

tracking to gutturally raw Elmore James.
He airguns water rats by a souped moat,

his deerhound Syphilis shampooed by spray…
His liquor intake's like a disappearing trick,

the measure of an invisible sea
that drops and rises trafficking empties.

He's the survival-paradigm,
not closed, but looking out, holding the flow

of hot riffs in his rivered blood,
pumping instinctual beat into a sound

building its own long-arc trajectory
over the waiting in five continents.

Solid Bass

He's triple c: Caroline, cavalier,
Charles II hairstyled,
deep-Englished

in propensities, eccentricities,
sunglassed, unaffected gecko
absorbing background naturally

and plotting mainstay chords
as though his bass is diaphragmed
as heartbeat to the song

auscultation
like hearing voices in a well
a deep down resonance.

He's chewing gum and high collars
Regency waistcoat coloured damson
his presence making inertia a style

of dispassionate statuary.
It's image, and he'll cook the girls
another hotel later,

get lipsticked like a horned bacchante
by the orgiastic.
Inscrutably no-give on stage

he's moated round, unreachable,
but there like foundations rooted
in an ivied manor.

He's ageless amongst 60s youth,
Rolls-Royced and diaristic,
band-chronicler writing it down

like a rock-history Tacitus,
the crazies, riots, outrage on the road,
the sheer unprecedented worship.

Courtfield Road

The sausage trampolines in fat,
fork-pronged cholesterol spatter
an ingenuous groupie twists
in sizzling batter—
a mid-morning brunchy affair,
the kitchen a graveyard of caked dishes
randomly highrised, gunked and slewed
to deviated minarets.
He's upstairs in the gallery
affecting a gold kimono,
cross-legged, his blue eyes cancelled out
by mental trouble, free-floater
hallucinatory tableaux.
Le petit mal dusts his aura
with disconnection, black-outs, faze.
He's deconstruction to himself,
his hand plotting a whisky glass
like complex chess played
with the bottle. Two tulle sunflowers
impose quasi-ecology
on the lowlight interior.
Brian tinkles a tambourine
to compensate for emptiness
with little twinkling flurries.
He feels like a light-exposed negative,
the image dematerialised
inside an ectoplasmic frame.
His crackly vinyls are de-sleeved,
clothes litter every chair, bright silks
and velvets ruined at the seams.
The groupie punishes his snakeskin boots,
bats at the fry-up's hissy squish
of popping frazzles, bacon, eggs,
a sunset-squally tomato,
pops buttons on a satin shirt
filched from a drawer, and contemplates
the maestro's used-up, flash-fired youth,

his untogether zero-impetus
keeping him moody, as she tips
anchor-shaped mushrooms on two raunchy plates.

Keith Richards' Rhythm Trick

A slide pickup in 1962,
a cheap f-hole guitar for trafficking
Chicago blues, Bo
Diddley, Chuck Berry, just paying dues
to growling blues myths, journeying

through Howlin' Wolf and B.B. King,
meshing with Brian's edgy chords,
lead and rhythm doing counterpoint.
Later the licks are open tunings:
D, A, D, F, A, D low

to high, like Twenties, Thirties blues,
nothing on paper, played by ear,
a high string tuned an octave lower.
style's his paterfamilias
grown in him like rings on a tree,

seasoned, understudied grain.
Tooling a Gibson J-200,
Nashville strung, a ringy 12-string,
he lays down at Muscle Shoals
Alabama, a feel-good, crisp

as crackly bacon 'Brown Sugar'.
Custom made by Newman Jones
his five-string guitar organises
huckster figures, aluminium neck
cushioned by red varnished maple.

Fingerprints with claw-hammer,
works a scorched little finger
playing bottleneck with glass
from a green Heineken bottle,
gets the sound with inimitable class.

Uses a small studio amp
to think big, and plots by ear
a pattern that gives infrastructure
to a phrase, and builds on it
his bluesy individual signature.

Neronian

Heliogabalus, Caligula, Nero,
despotic, transvestite psychos
fisting out jewels like Campana hailstones,

emeralds cool as deep water;
draggily made-up in ostrich feathers,
self-divinised, flexing a leashed leopard

en route to a same-sex sauna.
Heliogabalus peppers the 60s
with orgiastic aphrodisia

a Jagger/Richards/Jones androgyny,
bibbed satin shirts, UFO-like ascot hats,
a drug-fest saturnalia,

the limos stagy as hearses,
a rear-seat groupie ostentatiously
pouting with a red lipstick gash,

somebody spooning caviar
from its post-cryogenic state
into a slippery tasting palate.

Reckless excess in Chelsea,
Byronic lotharios in velvet
turn night into day with amyl nitrate,

eulogise the unending party.
Decadent patricians reincarnate
in the exalted glitterati,

the boy-gods stadiumed again
with feedback and a microphone,
like the Stones in a froggish armoured car

nudging to the swollen amphitheatre,
the crowds hysterical, the thrown roses
the sunset-red of the assassin's mark.

PURPLE HAZE

Jimi Hendrix

His body's a guitar anatomy,
the frets his vertebrae,
the stereo panning, his right and left
brain hemispheres in dialogue
creating fuzzy imagery—
feedback that roars like a hangar's
interior.
He deconstructs blues roots, freaks chords
to angry speed track dissonance:
a wall of sound Le Mans.
Jimi's the maestro sound-painting
at Record Plant, with the audacity
of a black Picasso
texturing customised riffs;
an iconoclast exploding colour
from the vibrato bar.
He tools purple off the taut strings,
coaxes an oscillating whine,
his Stratocaster twitchy as a horse
that won't be tamed. Tides lazily
turn over in his epic score,
as though this virtuoso played a beach
one haze-inflected rainy day.
A shattered aural collage, he retrieves
the fragments, builds a blue rainbow
over the soundscape's
gutsy ethereality,
or guns a strafed 'Voodoo Chile',
a cyclone packed into its core,
all sizzling wah-wah like a hex.
The work's a microcosmic artefact,
a guitar brain-scan, shamanic
conception, frantic by degrees,
then escalating to a solar storm.
His dark's an edgy form of light
illuminating everything,
his guitar hand sketching the moon and sun,
and reaching out into the galaxy
as though turning the stars on one by one.

Cream

Neocontrapuntal,
the ashcan drumming, jazz vocal,
wind-tunnel

sepulchral guitar
turns Robert Johnson's blues over
like a wave spilling treasure

across a roughed-up shore.
They cook with chillies; they're so hot
their phrasing's arson.

Clapton's apotheosised,
his broody licks are high voltage
stichomythia

haloed by cocaine.
Three mavericks hotchpotching rock,
they skew it tangentially

to a sonic World War 3,
a burnt out in the stratosphere;
music with a Frankenstein brain.

A self-destructing holocaust,
they oven 'Wheels of Fire'
like it's Shakespearean tragedy,

or introspectively capsule
inside 'White Room', feeding it jabs
of wall-eyed solitude.

All over London's underground
graffiti tags assert 'Clapton is God'
in shocking pink calligraphy,

referencing his power-points
and how the summer shines like tangerines
the volume up on 'Sunshine of your Love'.

Pink Floyd

Barrett's the madcap jumped out of the boat,
the microdot-svengali froggily
swimming the Cam in a red velvet coat,

searching for a drowned Alice in the stream.
On stage the music riffs psychotic core,
his Telecaster mapping out a dream

of space-time nomads exiled in the stars.
The band builds soundscapes round his rhythmic flux.
The UFO's lighting rig turns red like Mars;

his voice rips across tritons, flattened chords.
The cellar bleeds with urgent decibels
as Barrett hunts himself across the boards

framed in a groove that bleaches jazz of blues.
He's like a shaman swallowing the wind
to breathe into a tribe directional clues

to where the animals go down to drink.
He's theatre messing with reality,
his arched-back crawl or big cat's threatening slink

turned on the crowd as confrontational scare.
The rhythm section follow scattily
searching his aural footprints where they dare.

The club's a freaky pheromonal crush,
a blippy keyboard-textured mounting wall
of tensions hanging on the unleashed rush

of Barrett's energies, his improvised
sketches building to ethereal ascent
then smashed into a form to be reprised.

He walks off mid-number, slams his guitar
over an amp, then runs out into the night
leapfrogging over an obstructing car.

The Kinks

Post-Larkin and pre-Morrissey,
they talk up small despair, skin the apple
to aggrandise the worm,
unseam the cultural flaw, monotony
implanted in the humdrum like a loop—
a rusty Waterloo sunset
framed on commuters as an orange glow,
Ray Davies' sardonic commentaries
pinking the Top Ten, pickling irony
inside the deadpan lyrics, and the flat
underachieved delivery.
'Sunny Afternoon', 'Dead End Street',
the songs unhook pedestrianism
like a bra, find the nipple
standing up like a pasta twirl,
a bitterness implicit in the taste...
Quirky, placing cherries on the pop-cake
with doodles of icing-calligraphy,
they peaked with 'Lola', then went down
like a building swallowed by a lake,
old survivors romping in clear shallows
guitars strapped on their backs.
They're monoliths who stay around,
disinherited, repatriated
according to fashion, Ray's down-turned smile
admitting all achievement's lost and found.

Velvet Underground

That casual monotonal Brooklyn drawl
cross-pollinating drag
with Frank O'Hara's Lunch Hour Poems

a book that fits a jeans pocket
(City Lights 1959).
Lou's diffident camp innuendos—

the cocksucker in 'Sister Ray',
the sailor's hat in 'Heroin',
the fugitive in 'Waiting For The Man',

are closety pre-Stonewall nods
at gestative liberation.
He's mean, but soft inside defensive spikes.

His rhythm guitar's choppy, like someone
trying to balance in a skiff
rocked by groundswell.

Cale's his projected shadow, viola
shrieking dissonance: a musical assassin
raiding the studio for kill,

pitching subverted classical
against squalling feedback, his drone
emitting sonic voodoo.

Nico's so glacial, her crushed-ice tone
freezes mid-phrase,
solidifies around the lyric.

The backbeat's tom-tom hypnotic,
the songs alternate noise with calm
spilling like sunlight on an attic floor.

Lou's the monopolist, the plot,
the butch purveyor of an attitude
cool as a black Star & Frost diamond.

Traffic

Countrified in Berkshire, frisky corn
blading the skyline with blonde drowse
their soporific cottage hung over
by sunflowers, a giant race
flat-faced and blackly glowering;
they fuse pastoral with improvised sitar
inflect an R&B template
with Eastern shimmer: you can see for miles
their outdoor light-show rehearsals
strobing auroral patterns through the night,
orange and purple, blue and red
detonations in the dog-barking rural dark.
Hallucinogens, I Ching, the grass for nerves,
the wind as breath, rain as rhythm,
they're foxy shamen companioned by owls,
weasels and undercover stoats.
Winwood's the white soul voice in retinue
with Marriott, Burdon, jazzy Jack Bruce,
his diction rolling words like a freight-train
grainy with a choked-back lament.
The hits shimmer with psychedelia's
luminous blow balls 'Paper Sun',
'Hole in my Shoe' with its lysergic bestiary
shocked in the lyrics, 'Coloured Rain'
electrifying fuzzy vision.
They're of the moment for a year,
out in the sticks in a utopian oasis,
communal living, mostly high
in autumn from inspirational mushrooms,
drawing well water that contains the sun
like a cracked egg, a red concentric yolk
spilled in reflection, everything
simplistic, feathers in their hats,
and for a while their chart territory won.

THE BIG PINK

Blonde on Blonde

The Nashville sky's so zoom-shot clear
he sees the galaxy's gold shoulder
ray out stars.
Bob's songs are scraps made into isobars
of inspired moments, like his hair
curly as egg-whisked caviar.

He's hobo rough at the Ramada Inn
and menacingly AWOL
and dumb like it's amnesia,
writes lyrics on the hotel paper—
a crablike epithalamion—
the shuffling 'Sad-Eyed Lady Of the Lowlands',

done for Sara,
not the leopard in a tiara—
Edie Sedgwick,
her frontal lobes burnt by electric shock.
His song's a train pulling across America,
that long—11mins 23,

it hauls a shot to burning dictionary,
the words re-scrambled to explosive flame—
a Dylan book of Genesis.
Green Leprechaun cocktails do the trick
on 'Rainy Day Women 12 & 35'—
the lyrics stumbled over, the sound live

as sitting in a tiger's heart.
Bob's deep as Lake Ontario—
you get no feel of personality,
just the slurred improvisational maestro,
his verbal fluency like meltwater:
his skyline bumped into behind black shades,

the world ends in his lenses, flat
as a brick wall.
His sureness needs no rehearsal—
one take, you get it or you don't,
perfection won by carelessness
like a blind person catching a thrown ball.

Big Pink

A house the colour of a strawberry milk shake
out to grass at West Saugerties
($275 a month):
green leaf swimming into green leaf,
the silence empty as a Rothko:
Bob's baby blue dirt-crusty Ford Mustang

checking in at noon each day,
the maker turned punctilious worker,
carrying inspiration like a flower
(a blue iris) responsive to a bee.
He exits the car, a folky boho
flailing a mad dash through the racy shower...

He's poet in residence at Big Pink,
free-associating at a clumpy
key-clacking Olivetti typewriter,
lyrics biting chewed ribbon on the page,
the mishits, misprints over-underinked
in a liberally verbal diaspora

of vision opening windows on the day.
They're reefer-humour, songs jammed out
round laughter like the rising froth
on a poured beer—a carbonated head
that's like a frill. They're a basement quota
recorded on a two-track reel to reel

in cowboy boots and jeans that worn
they're like a patchy central marker line.
Bob calls the key and the Hawks improvise
surreal as a band picking flowers
inside a dream, sensual frisson,
with feeling notes to their organic roots...

They keep the windows open on the breeze
and full-throated magnolias look in,
a lilac like a purple elephant
tweaks a proboscis. Sunlight on the floor
does yogic meditation: the band laze:
time's like an insect settled on the skin.

It's happy days: Bob deepens his retreat:
the Woodstock recluse lost to green
proliferating thought off the highway,
cleans up his blood, stays in the quiet
apprehension of writing songs that seem
beautifully crafted as rough grained tree bark.

BREAKING A BUTTERFLY ON A WHEEL

Wormwood Scrubs

Richards banged up—the 19th century cell
sits on him like a concrete
turtle shell,

a chair, a pencil and paper
to write 'Dear mother,
da-da-da,'

his amygdala
switched to fear, a blunt-edged spoon
reflecting a tinny moon,

the little window set up high
admitting a blue rectangle
of cloudy summer sky

cancelled that afternoon to grey.
A lifer drops him tobacco—
a knuckle like a gold nugget

of Golden Flake; the prisoners rap
camaraderie on his door.
one year written on him like a tattoo,

he does compulsory in the yard,
the prison collects an eruptive roar
of stomping applause worked up floor by floor

for 'Satisfaction'. Mug shot done,
paranoia creeps like a waterline
notching up its ascendancy.

Later, the news: he's out on bail:
jump-starting freedom, kicking at the door,
leaving historic boot marks on the wall.

Brixton Prison

The fetid squalor has him gag,
the archetypal bad boy
used to a red leather upholstered Jag

monitored by a twitchy screw.
Jagger's the tiger in a cage,
stripped of his belt, bracelet and rings,

brushed by the warder's eye, as though
the man would beam him dead.
His pencil's the trajectory

to planets rayed across the galaxy.
He feeds the paper scrambled lines
of dithyrambic poetry,

flinches at his grey uniform,
scents danger in his cell-mate's
uncoordinated glower.

He's there for non-prescription speed—
four blue synergised offenders,
methyl amphetamine hydrochloride—

mother's little helpers.
He's wreckage, like a plane shot down
in free fall over London.

He's cut back, a cause célèbre,
fielded by Tom Driberg's pro-gay
defiance of the Commons…

Summer's outside like a silk dress
rewarding curves.
It's orangey 1967.

They work to get him out on bail.
Time's jumped ahead and he's behind,
busy again, anxious to sniff the real.

Robert Fraser

An aerospace silver Rolls-Royce
fins out of Mount Street, elitist chicanery
nosing it through a goldfish
red neon
in flashy Mayfair rain.

His chauffeur blindsides to the rear,
Mohammed with his oily curls
resembling black pearls,
clicks the door open at Duke Street,
umbrella open like a black pansy

showing a purple underside.
The gallery window's a concrete trip,
a psychedelically painted
AC Cobra sports,
all pink and orange paisley swirls

sprayed grasshopper green.
Warhol and Jim Dine on the walls;
the venue's ultra-hip.
Robert's red jelly old Etonian drawl
imparts a Fortnum's sheen

to every transaction.
Openings are faggy coteries
Jagger drops in on, camp in pink,
bad mouthing hubris as an act
like drugs and drink.

Robert's after hours Dilly boys
are blackmailing hustlers
shirted by Jeremy Thorpe…
They're straight, but play into the warp
as spotty painted toys.

Busted, his nerves reorganised
in Wormwood Scrubs, he hammed it up
as supplementary cook:
a cold turkey, squashed, premature dead act
biting on a thin nether lip…

Renascent, he partied all night
on credit and Chateau Petrus,
nibbled Beluga caviar,
a Stones aristo crashing out
the decade in a leather bar,

bankrupt from generosity,
surviving bailiffs' raids
to die wasted on AZT,
lungs full of plague and retroviral cells
christened as 1980s Aids.

ITCHYCOO PARK

I am the Walrus

Lennon's the acid prototype,
two microdots on Fortnum's caviar
nibbled off a recherché spoon,

the taste iffy, testicular.
Yoko wearing a wizard's hat
splashy with fat gold stars.

He's gurufied with alkaloids
coming up in his chemistry,
and in state at the Dorchester

sits lotused on the roomy bed
watching mosaics constellate
as though his brain cells were Big Bang

atomised across galaxies.
The rubber universe expands
in violet, blue and red.

They tweak each other telepathically
and share a thought's that binary
its impulse showing up the same

in a consensual flow.
He feeds lyrics to a tape recorder
haloed by a rainbow.

Everything's cosmic. When he speaks
his words float out like fish
sipping at current.

They sit together and apart,
magicking gestures, white-suited,
ashrammed on ritzy capital.

They're two, they're one inside the drug.
She places a cloud-shaped white rose
over his tantric heart.

Hang Fire (Europe 1967)

Brian's slinged arm's like a clubfoot
an orthopaedic jackboot
doing a clumsy thoracic salute.

At Malmo there's a riot
they slow by playing 'Lady Jayne'
like singing Thomas Wyatt.

Europe's student zeitgeist
pumps a batoned iron fist
at the bespoke and caviarred

Moet & Chandon commissar.
In Paris they're searched by a functionnaire
Smelling like a Pigalle bar's

stock of Provencal Ricard.
In Warsaw, riot police bludgeon
students like they're gutting sturgeon.

Honski de boyski boisk
zee Rollingstonzki.
Brian does his imitation Nazi.

Each border-check's an obligatory strip,
an unsanctioned mind-police
psyching into axons, dendrites.

A smoke bomb Etnas in the hall,
its mushrooming opacity
silencing the jungle roll

of Charlie's tribal bongo.
Their rhythm's the epicentre
of the revolution's core,

hot licked pounding incantations
feeding the molten tsunami
with a bushfire's thunder roar.

Torched

Monterey Purple's the acid head hit.
Hendrix works fuzzbox freakery,
kneels to himself as avatar
his torched guitar
roaring with lighter fluid

swung around his head and smashed,
re-launched on a trajectory
as meteoric dazzle.
The night burns like a mid-air crash—
Townshend auto-destructing his axe

curtained by a smoke-bomb.
Jefferson Airplane do hallucinogenic
opera, neural surgery
fine-tuned to the visual cortex,
leaking into the temporal lobes...

An epoch's re-contextualised
by how imagination colours
social patterns?—the event horizon
framed by the guitar hero
eviscerated on the stage

slit belly full of red roses
a floral hara-kiri.
It's 1967. Death
is accessed by LSD
and rehabilitated to the brain atlas,

a virtual state put on the map.
Poppies grew louder all that year,
red and translucent pink saucers,
the sunflower building high
and wide as the Pacific sky.

Nothing remains? The legacy's
assimilated by the loss,
the era beaten back by police
and guns and dogs, its energy
programmed into re-mastered CDs.

Odgen's Nut Gone Flake

Summer's a punt on a green pond,
four quirkies like water boatmen
zigzag a course through reedy silk
and stand under a willow tree.
An open notebook and a pen—

Steve fishes for a lyric theme.
Their raucous cockney pounds the air,
a bottle's thrown, a second one
describes a blunt trajectory:
the water spills a 3D glare.

They pole back into centre-stream,
picking chords for 'Lazy Sunday',
the impromptu music-hall voice
bricky with stoned delivery,
blueprinting it along the way.

The light's the colour of Chablis
raying the English afternoon.
A kingfisher's explosive flash
rips by: they beat out on the prow
the knuckled baseline to a tune.

It's 1967, time's
gone missing; a swan's angry stomp
beats water with percussive thrash.
They party impishly, someone
teeters, as though about to jump…

They loop the pond, a hat frisbees
into the glitter. Two songs down.
The sky turns frothy, dark violet
and orange clouds collect in shoals.
The hat's retrieved by its flat crown.

A concept's needed; a joint's fed
with Acapulco weed.
They argue credits noisily,
invent a marijuana brand
to touch down from a week of speed.

A carp nudges up, scenting rain.
They row a wobbly for the shore.
Their tape's eaten up by rewind ;
thunder's around, and midges ball
into an ovoid mass, then soar.

Hendrix's First

Pol Pot and Genghis Khan
Ku Klux Klan through the Marshall amps
scorching cycloned engineers.

Jimi's licks are live thunder
at De Lane Lea and Olympic
gizmoed by an airforce maestro

with electronic flap gear,
thick tones bled from overdriven
harmonics of the valve.

The man's an Afro on a hatpin,
a virtuoso cranking a Wagner scherzo
to shrieking psychedelia,

raiding Philip Jose Farmer
for sci-fi imagery,
blasting it like a meltdown in the sun,

a die-off of sound levels...
'Foxy Lady' burns testosterone,
'Manic Depression' rolls like a storm,

'Red House' dialogues blues chatter
across angry flight path roar,
like a Sten Gun fitted to an exhaust

for firing on the highway.
'Third Stone From The Sun' howls apocalypse,
hot as a crematorium oven

flashing mass to ash.
The cook-up's the title track's
backwards-effect solo,

the wonky piano out of tune,
the force-field instructing
a red sun risen from the sea.

Cohen's First Three

Hash smoke sits on his tongue like a yogi
shaped out of breath with foggy eyes,
raspingly aromatic body—

colouring vision, pointing up a tune
salvaged from downsides, stroking loneliness
to a responsive tingle of found chords.

He picks out melodies arranged
simply as wind-blown plum blossom
drifting across a Chinese poem.

His songs elevate sacrifice,
the letting go of love, the paring it
to something like a sculpted memory,

a fragile, coded signature.
He leaves them bleach like skeletons
left in the mountain furze by hawks

as calcified obituaries.
They turn moods over, like a train at night
heard from the corridors of sleep,

or like a ship's horn in a foggy bay
snowballs the listener's heart with loss
lemony as the harbour tang.

His voice lifts words like building-blocks,
they seem that heavy, phonemes cut
from a cliff-side quarry.

He sings to lovers on the other side of walls
and to the solitary who backpack off
in search of vision. His lines open out

the way we strip a sweetcorn of its sheath,
peel back the leaves to claim a maize
that's knobby as a golden honeycomb.

Brian Jones Trips

Psychotic repartee—
the drug answers back
in sci-fi imagery
excerpted from Mars?
as weirdly morphed scrambles

of panicked imagery.
His hand won't unclam
a Ventolin inhaler's
talismanic properties:
he digs in his hold.

The minder can't manoeuvre
Brian to his Rolls:
studio time is real time
he blankwalls, defers
the sleek haul to Barnes.

LSD's the crazies
to his zapped chemistry:
black popping spiders
laboriously track his skin
routing his epidermis

to find a way in.
He's bad-trip invaded
by arachnid avengers
little beady eyes
like headlights on his thorax

turning meteoric,
orange, yellow, red,
explosively eruptive,
the fire in his head
wind-stormed through the flat .

Visual turns audio
with voices in the pipes
natterishly conspiratorial
to his bubbling paranoia
they'll throw him out the window.

His cold sweat bumps hot
from psychoactive toxins,
Brian with a red guitar
and pink velvet suit
gesturally defensive

paralysed with fear
missing out another session
as virtuoso colourist,
already the delinquent,
gone missing, legendary star.

Satanic Advocates

Jagger's the morning glory vined
to a decade's toxicity
the chemicals grown saturnine,
spacily mind-altering
acid a visionary gateway

to the garden's underworld,
'Sympathy For the Devil's drapes
on mid-sixties floral pop,
all the dandelion-faced hippies
basementing themselves on smack

gone down a dark corridor
curated by the criminal
sunglassed insiders to the law:
Brian Jones undercover,
harassed, pushed into a fall...

The garden's lost its summer daze
its psilocybin rainbow
diffused over every park:
the King's Road darkens along noon,
something's waiting in the sun.

The Stones are blacker limousined
drugs and occult in their blood
Richards a ceremonial
cocktailer of substances,
curtains drawn across the day,

wasted, bean-stringy on speed.
Mostly it goes degenerative
the age's burnt neurology,
all its druggy casualties
sucked to a psychotic core.

The music's hard-edged, rockier,
rumours of disbandment, the blonde
retreating to a Cotchford farm,
death-bound, scenting day by day
his sacrificial murder.

Their Satanic Majesties Request

She heats a pin and sticks it through a doll
as crude voodoo, intestinal jab
that's gut and liver, imprecates his name—

the blonde one diabolised by her kink.
The band scratches at psychedelic-tech,
a fuzzy electronic vaudeville,

guitar-spook buried in mellotron swirls,
as though the prankster hidden in the song
was Humpty Dumpty sitting on a wall…

Court cases nagging in their nerves, they wire
their newly channelled Faustian energies
to off-tilt numbers, svelte Moroccan drums,

the apprehension of bells, rattles, gongs,
textural fade-out and fade-in harmonies.
The flavour's rainbow, churning blues and mauves

banded to citric orange, broody green,
an acid spectrum translating the times
to chemical palette, a jamboree

of wizards hats, faux magic cooked by drugs.
The music points a finger at its source
a rehashed Sgt Pepper lacking stripes,

a ludic playground romp, a finger wag
at the city's Square Mile. Now they invest
defiant image with experiment,

and cocktail tinkling flourishes around
a savage core, play with it and resolve
to kill the soft dynamic that they've found.

Tintern Abbey—Vacuum Cleaner

Ingenious high-octane psych,
infectious lustre, a sharp jewel

from the UK underground's apogee—
pyrotechnical 1967.

Deram experimentalists,
their one single so consummate,

it's coloured like an orange ice-lolly
with summer flavours.

Should have been a Number One
wired there by rooky guitar

and manic tail-chasing percussion,
a vocal like a down turned smile,

the bass-line subterranean,
the beat wackily asymmetrical

and driven like a stunt car in a yard,
but missed out in the plethora

of psychedelic overload.
three minutes of unrivalled pop,

catalogue number DM164,
the song was their obituary,

articulate and topical,
a model of its quirky genre,

alive today, as then, unstoppable
with red alert immediacy.

LUCY IN THE SKY WITH DIAMONDS

Rubber Soul

Pre-65
'the lyrics don't go anywhere'
(Dick James): they're lemon sherbet fizz
bagged from a provincial shop?
New York blacks out: a power cut
unplugging its diamond planet:

the President's caught right hand on his cock
in the invasive dark.
'Norwegian Wood' creeps by on the waters
as a first lyrical salute
to going serious, its quirks
displaying worry lines, its art

tweaked by a double-tracked sitar.
In London the Whitehall corridors
smell like a long-haul Boeing flight.
Lennon views Battersea Power Station
as a megalithic avatar:
an urban totem cool as a pop star.

The nights in 1965 are days
painted in Rothko tones. Plath's Ariel
explodes out of her suicide
as myth extracted from the mortuary.
Crows swoop rowdily on her publishers:
Faber & Faber 24 Russell Square.

Lennon goes deep on 'In My Life'
pulling the song's umbilical
out of a dream tied to red shoe laces
he couldn't knot at four.
His substrate's Menlove Avenue:
Liverpool graft, redundant, gritty, poor.

They lick their way through 'Drive My Car'.
George Martin hears them like a lost river
finally surfaced above ground.
It's always late at Abbey Road,
the studio burning money and their sound
coming on strong like a field of wild flowers.

Revolver

Rain's like the colour of meditation:
clear eye.
It scrolls liquid peas on the Albert Hall—
Dylan inside plugged into the low sky,
the Hawks (a.k.a. The Band) are thundery
companions to his songs stripped raw

as turpentine.
Lennon's found colour TV in his head.
He's filmed with Dylan's disconnect:
their Rolls swishing across Hyde Park,
their fusion unproductively
rehearsed on a moulded dark red back seat

big as a boat-sized Empire bed.
Geoff Emerick's tweaking tape loops
at Abbey Road, pop Berlioz
modifying through two Brennells
to do a space hop on 'Tomorrow Never Knows'—
the taped sound edited to itself

like an obsessional churning
the same thought while he burns his lip.
Lennon gets satori
by Marble Arch. Bob's shades don't leave his boot.
He's looking for a word coiled there
like a worm at a root.

They'd rather fly on a Persian carpet
clean over Buckingham Palace,
the thing undulating like a sting ray
through puffs of rolling cloud.
Back in the studio, George's sitar
inflects the ambitious essay

with saturnine kundalini.
Their instruments list like a found poem:
Paul's Epiphone Casino,
Harrison's short-scale Burns Nu-Sonic bass
and Gibson SG, Lennon's Gretsch Nashville
all mesh together on 'She Said She Said'.

Revolver's not a smoking gun;
it's summer pop turned tricky for its good
with an arpeggiated glow.
Lennon and Bob sit still beneath a tree.
The camera shoots time on the lifting breeze
raising the dust; the moment come and gone.

Sgt Pepper

You could read Ballard's Disaster Area
listening to the Edwardian variety
orchestra's

jamboree fusion with heavy rock—
the Beatles' Sgt Pepper
symmetrical

as the haemoglobin molecule,
snazzy as boatered music hall,
colourful as a spill of Smarties

tap-dancing into a cupped hand.
How many holes fill up the Blackburn road?
Less than the two million hydrogen atoms

grouped on a full stop.
The songs radiate shimmery aura
yellow as a 1967

St John's Wood rayed-out dandelion
lifting a head at Abbey Road.
The melodies seem up there in the sky

like Lucy. You could sit all day
and treat the music as a happening:
a drug-dream floating by like last night's sleep

seen as a hazy tableau on the lake.
Toot. Toot.
Telepathy's their shared gestalt:

it leaks out of the speakers, varispeed.
You could read Philip Dick's Counter-Clock World
listening to 'A Day in the Life',

everything new, open and possible
as quantum stuff, or take up the reprise
that's abstract, almost mystical.

Abbey Road

Apple eats credit like a killer star
a rogue black hole in Savile Row,
its gut deep as the Underground.
Money for pop's like a gang heist,
the loot channelled by middle-men
tricky as branch lines in a reptilian

cardiovascular system.
The end's a blow out—Abbey Road
plum with its cute arpeggios
and bittiness, like late sunlight
locked into haze, as a decade
shatters inside a studio:

a rooftop concert blown away
by four Rishikesh prodigies
bearded like fakirs in the cold
blue brunt of frosty January,
all Jesus hair and disconnect,
excessive fame worn like a permatan

on a Scouse Eskimo.
Inside the boot, a purple sock
is holed by John's obtrusive toe...
They group together for humour
or point up solo
'The Ballad of John and Yoko'.

'Here Comes The Sun's' an optimistic breeze
as the Apollo hits the moon
July 1969.
Music doesn't save anyone?
Agent Orange fries Vietnam.
Lennon's bass-chords plod out of tune

on 'The Long and Winding Road'.
They're disappearing into self belief
as a corrosive myth—
four limos separating across town
in August swelter—it's behind them now
the sun that's so much redder going down.

White Album—The Beatles

Abbey Road, Studio 2,
the friction's like a reactor:
Yoko sits in a lotus pretzel
holding a white carnation,
perched on the piano while John
drives into 'Sexy Sadie'.

They're post-Maharishi converts
sold on the East, open to
meditating on the Ganges
as the river in their blood:
but pin rebellion like the Iron Cross
on a blousy kaftan.

Disparately together,
their camaraderie's holed,
shot through like a fighter aircraft,
but tenaciously reassembled
on 'Back in the U.S.S.R.'
fuelled as a stompish killer.

1337 days
piecing kaleidoscopic fragments
into thirty incompletions,
a collage of minimal constructs,
the band breaking up, breaking down,
sold on solo excursions.

Their plot unfolds like the I Ching,
grass growing between the pages,
summery lives starting to seed
like thistle-glitter on the wind:
'Happiness is a Warm Gun'
blowing pieces out of the mind.

The work's a pastoral opus,
bitty, but opening out
like a field of gorgeous poppies
in which four eccentrics
make cartwheels around a piano
in the orange September sun.

Last Exit

At Chappell Epstein makes a last exit,
a decommissioned manager,
he looks like someone who's air-sick,
panicky, pill-faced and dysfunctional,
now touring's off schedule.
He leans in a dark suit against the wall,

brutally self-conscious he's queer
as pink, a brand name eating him
like depleted uranium.
Oppressive, fugitive, the studio's
alien to him—it's a sounds lab
for backward tapes and whimsically surreal

M.C. Escher staircases of see-sawing chords...
Depression's in him, flat and dark
as an unconscious reservoir.
He's made it fast. His screw up's personal.
Blackmail: a cottaging faux pas?
The decoy knew him in the rank pissoir...

His boys do custard pie lyrics:
a walrus wallowing in green slop pie:
a raft of clotted imagery
John free-associates at the piano.
His input's out. Time seems too real,
as though a crisis in his nerves

alerts him to his sparkly Dior watch.
He points a little finger when he smokes,
the way an actress does. His MBE
feels like the clunky Iron Cross.
They've come so far in five years, it's the moon
they've trodden on. Gain bleaches out as loss.

His cigarette's like a red camera lens.
He activates the sparky cone
dragging it to a furry bitter end.
He's Nems, the Cavern, but he's lost his glow.
He's still the faggy correct manager
turning his back on 'Your Mother Should Know'.

Brian Epstein

The curtains drawn all day at Chapel Street
on the residual blues. Last night's rent boy
left burn-marks peppered on the linen sheet.

He makes things happen between John and Paul:
his charm's infectious, and it colours deals.
Managing a rock band seems like long haul,

fielding the tacticals from EMI,
shaping an image—cooky ties and suits:
the limit's ten miles higher than the sky.

The bottle's half empty or it's half full,
a drinker's puzzle: he can't get it right.
The pills are gravity-free in their pull.

Sometimes his eyes are puffed up black and blue
from rough trade reprisals: the money talks,
then boots and knuckles claim an overview.

The night's his hunting ground; an unlit pier,
or West End casino, his jaw rattling
over baccarat or chemin de fer.

His need's for love, when same-sex is a code.
The pimply trick he turned at Leicester Square
had little gestures of camp overload.

The band won't tour: he fears redundancy,
internal fighting. Sometimes things explode
inside his head, and leave no memory.

Chocolate digestives by the bed: the boy
he hoped would stay, left nothing, no address,
just matches, and a used bottle of Joy.

This time it's pills he gambles: live or die?
Their dull eruptions happen in his brain.
His shirt's still on, so too his knotted tie.

ON THE BEACH

Brian Wilson at South Bay

His voice breezes on Hawthorne Boulevard,
cloning falsetto
with the stereo,
his itchy sunset-red Chevy
on flat out attack to the beach,

his pitch etherealised
on any treble peak.
A spacey sky with drop-by clouds
is 1963 Pacific blue:
backgrounded surf in scampering tempo

beaching as iridescent swash.
Safari-surfers at South Bay
are doped on Acapulco weed.
Parked up he grabs a frosty Coke
to feed him zingy energies,

and stares out at the crest-riders
skating blue sticks on the wave's arc,
measuring balance as the force
accelerates and in its rush
scuttles a board into free fall...

He's here to score, cruise the Witch Stand,
lyricise hymns to car-culture—
Little Deuce Coupe, Corvette Sting Ray,
a chromed up Ford, dragster Grand Prix,
he busies pop into his nerves

by menuing names for a song.
It's 'Surfer Girl' he bittily
constructs in scrambled imagery,
eyes spaced towards the tumbling surf's
distinctly modern dialect.

The hotdog settles in his gut
as calorific filler to his need.
He stands a long time looking out
at a new age arrive, jumps in
and segues back home at mad speed.

Procol Harum—A Whiter Shade of Pale

Will Shakespeare hauled out of the froth
for soapy lyric allusions,
a seaboard song, its theme wears ruffs

like an Elizabethan.
The bass-chord's all descent, the long way down
to drown

inside a vortex.
The organ's wash builds deep sea-swell
around the voice as though pitching a hull

in rolling undertow,
the ship sighted as hallucinatory,
so near or far, it's never there.

Getting wrecked is amnesiac,
a white on white bleach out of clarity,
the ceiling and the floor dissolved

along a seamless line.
'We skipped the light fandango,'
the crisis gaining—the sixteen vestals

available inside the maze,
or in the stateroom, white skirts like petals
revealing, but illusory.

We're never told of their identity,
the enigmatic caste, faces dusted
like actors in Kabuki?

The ship's part of the eternal return,
no touch-screen navigation, no radar,
its name wiped, and the foggy sea

collusive with the party going on,
all night, all year, the boundaries disappear
like UFOs as disinformation.

Living Fast, Dying Young

Summer's a beach tilted towards the sky,
a Beatles number stereoed from a car,
an oak tree's inviting bottommost shade
measuring out cool radius,
its jagged circumference like a star

laid flat in the breeze-skittish grass.
Somebody's picking a guitar
for tuneful dialogue, an extempore
way in for voice, a catchy sketch
worked from a hurt into a clear,

a plaintively phrased register...
He posts his back against warped grain,
his friends are up there in the hills,
bandanas, Hondas, bravura,
they signal their camaraderie

to other members of his band.
A burnt out decade lists its casualties—
a bibulous death-hexed Jim Morrison
a panicked Pan-like Brian Jones
the fuzzbox-oracle Jimi Hendrix,

rock-luminaries de-realised,
re-grouped inside the underworld,
their myths translating back as the returned,
the dead detained as the undead,
reconstituted by their sounds.

The band assemble in mid-field,
scaring up a folk elegy,
a song about a ruined youth, his bad
gone worse in jail, his open mouth
wounded with poppies and cornflowers.

The breeze thwacks grassy panicles,
its sorting done low to the ground.
Apple-blush cows amble upslope,
the music fetching, carrying
the scratchy impulse of a hit.

They jam, and lie back in the grass,
soaking up quiet. An epoch
expires in lazy cowbells, death,
its ideals deconstructed, trashed
by regenerative militancy.

Clouds build a high rise monument
over the scene. They up and leave,
wading waist-high through history,
their moment incomplete, their song
waiting to grow into a big event.

Brian Wilson Freaks

The airport washroom goes tumble-dryer.
The mirror blobs him. He's standing on swell
as though a ship rolled in jittery calm.
His off-white sneakers leak a cupboard smell.

Panic is the intruder in his cells,
pre-flight misgivings, hints of betrayal,
a wobbly skin-peeled vulnerability,
working him to a surface where it's raw.

Five minutes out of LA it begins,
a wolf's howl barked at 20,000 feet,
a convulsively slow-release debacle
of locked in mania starting to free

in crumpled spasms... He's mobbed in his seat,
the intravenous drug smacking him numb
as though a jeep working a gradient
cut out, wheels churning in impacted sand,

the drive gone dead, bodywork shuddering.
Later that night he's returned to LA
and sees the airport swarmed by jellyfish,
undulant floppies looking like they're lungs.

He's disbanded, and goes into retreat,
builds an artificial beach in his room,
the piano legs buried in grainy sand,
its mineral glitter catching at his feet...

He pulls out slowly, but the damage stays
like something hidden in a corridor,
a shadow turning over in his blood...
He leaves wet footprints on the sandy floor.

Surf Talk

An onshore wind cruises Pacific rush—
summers unfolding, sun-block, shades,
a generation sitting in the light
as so immediate a group
they seem the future lived by everyone

without die-off or change.
It's circa immortality,
the beach ethos soundscaped by surf,
youth identified by stretch marks—
a bikini's snappy vocabulary,

and somewhere back of it, tremolando,
the Beach Boys surfing vibrato
to workable strawberry-flavoured pop,
wind-movies caught up in the sound
and a surfboard's ethereality

tilting direct into the sun.
So many stepped out of the wave
fried by a self-destructing need,
got burnt and refocused the world
as water collapsing in blue 3D…

Summer spotlights each new decade
in ultraviolet, infrared,
the Beach Boys dropping in again
as disembodied revenants
falsettoing down the airwaves

a mantric, light-transparent chant…
The dead are windowed in their songs
like fractals spaced by harmonies,
their melodies evoking youth
drying red beach towels in the sun,

surfily stoned and bleached by salt,
doing a drug and out of it.
The sea picks bodies off its back,
returns them to the shore, dumps waste
like evidence against a crime

of universal toxic spill.
It's like percussion, choppy waves
running so fast a board picks up
a car's dynamic, chops it through,
the surfer thrashed by blinding spray

and hanging there on overreach,
balanced the way a generation dies
with music as its legacy,
but keeps on coming down the years
as voice-association to the beach,

a surf-talk mantra, doo-wop pitch,
the Beach Boys floating on the air
in vocal arcs, holding a place
in memory, as white thunder
lifts with its hard explosive glare.

MEMO FROM TURNER

Skewed

Brian's guitar-dead. His fingers bleed
on picking. A foundation smear
smudges peach on black cashmere
like a residual meteor
got by putting on a face.

He crashes from another space
disorbiting into orbit.
His lisp has a fur collar
like pussy willow.
He's pieces that no longer fit.

He's tea and drugs at four.
A China White Point and strawberries
peppered with hash.
His public school entourage slum
in Chelsea on trust funds and stash.

He's six years old inside his head,
blows harp into a microphone,
but gets no sound,
spends three capitulatory hours
putting a reed into a saxophone.

Vodka's like his swimming pool
a recreational gateway to
seeing things down under.
He tastes Russia in each antiseptic hit
and its moon-sized rye estates.

He's a passenger in a band
harnessed to global long haul.
He's snitched his tie in raspberry yoghurt.
Sometimes he can't separate out
the use of a foot from a hand.

He's fame and pins it on his sleeve.
His birthday cake's shaped like a pink gravestone.
He parties with it, it's pink snow,
goes back to Olympic and finds
he's locked out of the studio.

Crossfire Hurricane

They're punked-up, rebarbative
energy-hustlers;
Jagger's market stall bawl—'it's awwright'—
and it's hot
a lyric that's snarly, stroppily themed

from a Shakespeare plot
a volume turned up
Tempest rehash, a body fished out
on a desert island, beached
and reborn

with recalcitrant lip.
The singer's complaint's invective
in descant,
a post-spike-through-the-head
resurrection, off-centre sung

vituperative whiplash
at a vampirical mother
her witchy antics
zapping his genes,
but still imparting flash

to his hotwire recovery...
The riff's authentic smart,
so driven in
it hurts with neat authority,
so hooky it's on save

as instantaneous catch.
The band in execution
cut it clean
as laser surgery, a phrase
stitched into memory,

a two-chord carnal mantra
pumping like adrenalin.
They're in their moment, on its rush,
and can it 1968
as a compact exigency—

a three-minutes rock novella
chaptered as aural synthesis,
a streamlined waspish guitar bash
laying it down explosively
for vocal kill; Jumping Jack Flash.

Beggars Banquet

A muddy current permeates the blues,
a raw earth country flavoured undertow
chopped by guitars into a racier

discourse with life picked out along a seam
of youth resisting age, rejecting death,
confused, churned up, but finding clarity

in texturing a song with overbite.
Brian's a stress-bleached hoodoo effigy
shot through with hex pins, propped in a booth,

his bottleneck narrating rooty chords
dragged out like water-lilies from a pond,
notes bleeding in a black mood finale.

Mostly nocturnal work. Olympic. Barnes.
The register's a pummelled knucklish swipe
at hierarchy: they cut it fast and slow,

these brash reminders they are like a sea
advancing on the age, deep tidal push
smashing the props from 1968...

'No Expectations' bares a skeleton,
it's Brian's riff picks flesh off his bones,
as though he played by ear posthumously.

Richards lays skewed foundations to each song,
a schema for the singer's overview
in claiming luciferian attributes,

a quippy, giant-arena metaphor
for burning hot, shouldering a decade
and riding it out like a meteor.

Olympic Studios (Left on the floor)

A cache of misfits, stop and start
late night Jagger/Richards out-takes,
canned imperfections, raw
try-outs, a stoned 'Dear Doctor', furred
'Blood Red Wine' 2am muddied

by off-kilter savvy.
A 'Jumping Jack Flash' 1&2
don't meet it square, but miss nailing
the saturnalia with a riff
clean as a shark's grin.

A bootlegger's stock exchange sting,
the numbers go disowned and stay
as a completist's legacy—
a straggly 'You Got The Silver'
cat-licked to numbness by Jagger

as though he'd caught the mouse
and let it go.
A high octane 'Downtown Suzie'
is so tricky its dynamic's
wacky as robo-soldiers

able to shoot round corners.
Hear a floor-crawling 'Sister Morphine'
still half-cooked, its subject messed
on mainlining, Chelsea's own
disingenuous Marianne.

'No Expectations' as a rough
isn't personalised by Brian's
valetudinarian slide,
his spooky figures conjuring
imminent ruin, absent here.

Nights at Barnes, limos parked up
under 1968 rain.
The songs left over are eponymous
reminders of the lost and found
Decca dispossessions that still remain.

Going Down

Bare torso, pink scarf tied around his head,
Mick dances his shamanic Nijinsky—
L'Apres Midi d'une Faune electrified

by blasting rock in the full length mirror
at Cheyne Walk. He attacks like a whip,
then draws back, teasing like a pouty rose.

The room gives on the river's shimmered lick,
all Moroccan textiles and purple drapes—
tricked out for an odalisque on majoun,

its Ali Baba glitter themed by hash.
His inamorata's on messy drugs
and cheats on him to score each frozen shot

that sends her crashing lights out on the bed.
A snaky wisteria trails a plait
of festooning reminders down one wall—

shy smoky-blue flowers ruffled into frills.
Mick's a midnight to six studio jinn
lashing a lapsed band's fuddled energies

into coherent jams—they tape the lot—
Ry Cooder's figures inked into the mix
like permanent tattoos, slide artistry

coloured like Rimbaud's vowels in analogue...
A miscarriage, a film that's done for real—
Cammell tirading mania on the set,

the band re-train direction, get a nose
for criminality, the underside
of London's skin, the Kray hegemony,

the back end of Portobello, and twist
hard drugs into the wiring, blow the lid
on their mythology and give it blast.

Street Fighting Man

The river's filming 1968
as peripatetic cloud lucks over
at Cheyne Walk; a wobbly cumulus

detaches for the Chelsea Harbour build.
Summer smells of blackcurrant: buddleia
pokes purple tusks around the garden house

where Jagger's pop edge raps 'Street Fighting Man'
against Keith's beating-to-quarters chord riff—
the lyric heat-curling with insolence,

driving a revolution to its feet?
They feel their interactive flow, the power
go deep river with psychic energies,

even the song's unstructured rudiments
hinting at action poetry,
a snarlishly wolf-slinky signature

exhorting life in a rock n' roll band.
The tryout's buzzy like a chocolate fix
kicking in endorphins: the hook has bite

and streetwise savvy at its core.
London's its generative firepower.
They try it folksy, bluesy, wack it rock

and feel the playback hang like flame.
They've hit the moment with their anti-war
vehemence, lifted youth the right way up

to burn a flag and overturn the state...
They break, and feel the sticky heat oven,
July forcing the honeysuckle's scent

to gorgeous assault, and the future theirs,
hot for the taking, while the sky chokes up
with amazing sculptural slow-roller clouds.

The Rock & Roll Circus

Jagger's the dressy spiritus rector—
the whip hand ringmaster, his act's on cue.
Support's from the arena fire-eaters—

a mega-explosive rock-opera Who,
Townshend's molten windmilling power chords
fulminating like he's plugged into the sun.

John Lennon's skewed maverick Dirty Mac
cobble 'Yer Blues' round Clapton's grilling licks,
Yoko bodybagged into a black sack

at Lennon's feet like a dead artefact.
The cast are a decade older, wear tracks:
their arteries are gummed with sticky plaque.

The Stones come on to a ballsy 'Jack Flash',
long curtained hair, capricious, arrogant,
their yardstick's doing wind-ups in the face,

infamously diffident, couldn't care,
the singer shaking ass like a stripper,
fixing the camera with a cobra's stare.

They slow the tempo, Brian's wolfish slide
bleeds into a jittery epitaph—
'No Expectations' and he's terminal—

his pulse measured in each trembling figure.
They build to a macumba 'Sympathy',
a conga-driven litany to waste—

Mick whip-lashing his body like a snake
sticking its prey, then doing a board-crawl—
125lbs of electrified tissue,

amino acids, salts, Artaudian screams,
his satanic persona turned scary
as though he'd really do it in the street.

The Big Splash

A busted spine-strafed Penguin Brighton Rock
sits face up in the Redlands spill
of loony clutter—Keith's rehab centre—

one nervy day in 1968,
the band convening, while Ry Cooder's slide,
an open G tuning (five strings only)

morphs 'Sister Morphine' with an eerie tweak
of impetuous eloquence.
A brandy-wiped, redundant Brian Jones,

sits nonplussed, eye-bagged on the red sofa,
too uncoordinated to pick chords.
The clouds are origami postcard stuff

Greene might have eyed when writing Brighton Rock.
Brian's hysteria's like fizz shaken up,
the cork popped on the bottle by arrest,

his court case imminent, he starts to blow
in fuming paranoid snips, lashes out
at Jagger's bitchy, bee-stung flippancy,

picks up a knife and runs out to the lawn,
screaming he'll kill himself, bolts for the moat,
bleached hair tousled and flying burnt pink vents,

his rage proportionate to the green thrash
he makes in arcing through the scummed veneer,
frog-kicking as he spraddles in the slime,

a wheezing upended amphibian,
boots wedged in Jagger's palms, wrenched out face down,
shocked but still kicking, like a giant pike

pulled from the weedy murk and cursed by Mick
for dirtying his hands—his velvet suit—
his temper shouting there's no going back.

Memo from Turner

A psychosexual lab at Powis Square,
outside, offset, Keith Richards mits
his faux leopard-skin steering-wheel,
fogged out by smoke inside his car,
he beats time like he raps guitar,
jealousy knotted in his fist

at Jagger's boss-cat sexual fest
with his trashy sleep around:
Pallenberg doing it for real
with Mick's reactor-like libido
hot as the Amazon basin, steamy
as a flickery liana.

The shooting frames the 60s live,
the studied rock star shadowed by gofers,
Kray-links, bespoke gangsters in spotty ties,
East End yardies snowed on cocaine,
dodgy low lifers working for the Stones
like sticky bees around a hive.

The new aristos in their ecosphere,
Mick's hair is swishy Elvis-black,
his sexuality so epicene
he dissolves boundaries, swims through the two girls
and out again, a hologram
with a man's front, a woman's back.

The gangster taking refuge in the den
stays quizzical and angular,
rough edges teething like a saw.
He's straight, but colours like Pernod
with orange juice, resists, but spikes
the cocktail with a drinking straw.

Mick calls the shots. A magus holding court,
his slippery epigone at his feet.
A decade muddies like a Rolls-Royce hub,
violence integrated into its nerves.
His lips are glossed, his manicure complete.
He struts his bi-stuff through the druggy fort.

Whose execution is prepared by this?
We don't see clearly who's inside the car
slicing a line through 1968;
the limo bashed away from a neat square,
the ritual victim silenced, and its thrust
picking up speed across Notting Hill Gate.

Ladbroke Grove

Back of Portobello and Holland Park
a sort of miniature Haight-Ashbury,
a hippy microcosm's roomed up there:

a basement's diagrammed with mandalas,
lowlight lairs for the stoned inhabitants
staring into the semi-dark like toads.

A Jimi Hendrix poster maps the wall
in citrus-coloured fractals, orangey
star clusters mapped into cerise.

Community's the new grass-roots ideal:
money's designated as dead traffic,
like plaque gunking stiff arteries.

Macrobiotic ethics. East meets West.
Lentils, split-peas, Tao gastronomy,
each grain of rice repatriates a cell

to optimal longevity.
Honey's the alchemical elixir,
Pythagorean food for pacifists,

hash-eaters, fogged by joss-stick nebulae.
The future's present. Live in it and learn
about time's elasticity

is what they preach; and music amplifies
the moment, heightens its ingredients:
Bob Dylan inventing myth with each line.

They're family, grouped around the market's pull,
and bond there in a common need for dope,
granny's discarded mink, or just the high

that comes from searching on a Saturday
for faded things down Portobello Road,
and giving to their tarnish a new shine.

Growing up with the Voice

An oracular tutor
the voice brought deserts to my room
ash deposit from Dachu
and mountains where the visionary
tracked steps up a gold ladder.

Grainily avuncular
Leonard Cohen stepped into
my death-wished, shrink-wrapped youth,
serenely colouring each phrase
a rainy Sunday blue.

Omniscient in overview
his vision tightened in my nerves
Songs Of and Songs from a Room
arranged like mental furniture
in my backbrain.

Intimately familiar
I personalised his in-head tone
his voice rivering dead lovers
to a subterranean pool,
Hitler browsing in its depths

with a froth of rootless flowers.
His lyrics came as sanctuary
to those roomed in solitude,
losers learning how to win
from signs dictated by the rain.

Lacking confidantes, I chose
Leonard as adopted friend,
father to my outlawed state
as a poet, avatar
to my crumpled blue raincoat:

lived with him inside my pain
in my foggy harbour walks
round a maritime complex,
emptiness sounding my veins
like a foghorn in the bay.

Years later that trust resides
like a psychic monument
dissolved in a deep space in me,
Leonard's chargrilled baritone
cooking ascetic gravity.

The voice will follow to my end
as archetypal consoler
something like an aural hand,
that grabbed me once, and still persists
in pointing out the promised land.

LSD

The Doors of Perception

The crystals look like snowflakes in free fall
mescaline dissolved in a water glass
for Huxley's trial and error trip,

the LA morning blue with postscript smog
fluffing the San Bernadino valley.
Grey squares come up, a geometric grid

visually sequenced, with sometimes a blue
windowing possibilities, a pink
open the way a morning glory shows.

He half-trips, stalling on the drug's autonomy,
his flannel trousers turning grainier,
the texture breathing like a porous skin.

Structure breaks down into smart molecules,
boundaries lose edge, and now he's spatialised,
he strokes time like the soft fuzz on a peach.

Everything comes up patterns, and his friend
directs him outside, where a loaded vine
is seeded with gold planets, grape by grape,

suns blazing through translucency of skin.
The fig tree's vertebrae are like his spine,
a ladder pushing to connect with light.

He sees now without edits what's around,
the universal clarity of things
each polished to a bright immediacy,

as though a lemon swum into his eye
and kept on polishing, until it claimed
a singular visual consistency.

He goes back in, his altered state alert
first to particulars, and now the whole
turning a light on in him like the sun.

Brotherhood of Eternal Love

Farmhoused at Santa Ana, they magic
artichokes from inhospitable soil,
seed pumpkins redder than red mandarins,

and monitor the dirt road from a tower.
A hippy, altered state community,
they tune on orange sunshine, a kilo

of pure acid converted into hits.
Fuzzy utopians, they trip all day,
auditing drug-restructured chemistries.

Their bottom line's turn on the universe,
sugar-cube cognoscenti lending myth
to simple actions, like halving a fruit

to startle at the risen sun inside.
A truck chokes on a rocky hairpin jag,
its acid haul camouflaged by egg-plants.

The driver stops by. He's from Anaheim.
He travels with a discoloured I Ching,
boards warped, blue tattered jacket sun-bleached grey.

He helps unload into a green tepee,
jokes how the GIs slush through Vietnam
systems spiked by endemic LSD.

He makes a girl, then lopes into the hills,
scouting for saucers, reported sightings,
high on the space-inflected cosmic hum.

The acid buffs sample the potent strain,
play air guitar to Grateful Dead solos,
and bake a pumpkin for the man's return,

the lid scalped, contents spiked with rosemary,
and sit around its ceremonial
a fire bucking antlers at the first stars.

Hold Up

Sand and Scully Scully
and Sand
in their illicit partnership
keep synthesising LSD
for the revolutionary hip:
lack of ergotamine tartrate
substituted by methedrine
and still the purest
LA cut.

A Hell's Angel injects ante
hot on a courier's tail
bike kicked to a demented howl
grip biting on the coastal strip
the speedometer jammed
like the tank might explode:
'wheels of fire
rolling down the road',
it's Dylan's scorched eschatology
burning holes in his head.

He parallels
at 45 degrees, segues
across the rider's path, a cosh
raised in his leather fist,
forces the man into a ditch
orange with poppies, pulls a gun
and frisks his stash.

Sand and Scully Scully
and Sand
in their illicit partnership
manufacture ten million hits
of acid to turn the world on
to altered states, a chemical
theatre of psychodynamic play
everyone dreaming with their eyes open
on a violet and orange summer's day.

Stanley Augustus Owsley III

Ex-Air Force
radar buff, back from a high desert plateau,
   drunk on blue sky
and psilocybin, he's seen fighter jets
   de-realise on course
for base, synthesised lysergic monohydrate,
   and learnt to fly,
this time by rotating on the side chain
   of the LSD molecule,
tamping with structure to release the rip
   in psychotropic chemistry,
the mind unfolding like a butterfly,
   dotted with cosmic bintra.
An altruistic alchemist, he feeds
   his batches to community,
labs in a garage beneath white bug lights,
   a guttural vacuum pump
supplying its underworld commentary.
   His head's wrapped round
the Grateful Dead, their undulating chords
   cloning the drug's
own mechanistic, its internal sound.
   He contacts local radio
to have the DJ match his synthesis
   with acid-rock
mandalas, mind-bending guitar spirals,
   and works all night
stoned on the dusty penumbra rising
   like a benevolent mushroom
from a self-devised tableting machine.
   Later, indoors,
he'll sit naked on a leopard skin chair,
   hair-dryer in one hand,
discoursing on Chinese rugs, or a scent's
   peculiar anatomy,
his erudition wide-screened as the drug,
   his pet owl sitting somnolent

on a flamboyantly rainbow coat-stand.
Scully moons, talking of the take-over,
    drug-tactics going guerrilla,
LSD as the endemic payback
    for nuclear fission.
Neuronal architects, they work to split
    the brain cells like an atom,
fire STP into the chemistry
    as super-psychedelic.
They rap the morning through, the diamond light
    tooling a Ming Vase blue and red,
point Einstein's physics into chemicals
    and late afternoon go to bed.

The Byrds—Eight Miles High

Altitude's
in their chords, the clear air miles
  McGuinn and Crosby
open out, like a jet's contrail
  cooling to a white freeze.
They're space-rock prototypes,
  reaching for the blue sky -
a space inside and out, all boundaries
  dissolved.
They try for vertical axis
their climbout harmonies
giving 'Fifth Dimension' a spacier
  graft for quantum leap
out of the universe. Their throwback days
  as aviation fans
under the jet stream at LA airport
  return impressionistically;
a 12-string Rickenbacker colouring
  the melody
on 'Eight Miles High'. Their songs are voyagers,
  baselines
to go it interplanetary; prompters
  to NASA
to payload out beyond the solar belt.
  Mid-air's
their resting point, an ascendant
  maintained
by graduating arpeggios two miles higher
  than aircraft fly,
they level out at eight; the studio
  glossy with moon-shots
Blu-Tacked to blue sound-insulating walls.
  The sky's
their sound-board, fluffy cumulus
  vaporising between the lines
like snowflakes dusted off the skin.
  They're fine

as Californians tune, coasting the charts
   etally
then touching down to indigenous
   'Wild Mountain Thyme',
as though waking brushed by purple heather.
   Aero-space rock,
they underplay its streamlined energies
   diffident, cool,
but focused in their easy, laid-back way,
   casual
in flight, like pilots switching to remote,
   the sky
around them blue and settled for today.

Timothy Leary At Millbrook

Learning to fly
on psilocybin—he's lodged in a tree
sprung from his biology,
the leaves are cells, the trunk his vertebrae,
the primal soup the energy

by which he touches corners of the sky.
Everything's bright
and Blakean, in its psychoactive glow.
He sits in a rainbow
amazed how atomised photons of light
keep up an instructive flow
of data seen independent of sight.

Millbrook's the place—
a mansion lit by ice-floe chandeliers,
the hippy volunteers
caught in the coloured whorls of inner space
appear to disappear
inside hypnotic vision without trace.

The Persian rugs
present mandalas in each floral strip
bright colours rivalled by the trip
from cocktails of hallucinatory drugs
that by degrees start to unzip
neurons, like fire signalling between logs.

Sophist-guru
he wants to infect the water system
with LSD mayhem,
go global with the psychotropic view
like chipping a modem
to interact with the chemically new.

He colour-codes
breakfast as green scrambled eggs, violet oats,
        and bread as black funeral boats
launched on a rocky table that explodes
        with flowers: cats and dogs and goats
file through the hall. The DMT implodes.

        They sit around
composing renga, each makes up a line,
        the poem taking shine
as the invention of collective sound.
        Outside, autumnal pine
write airbrushed calligraphy on the ground.

        A funhouse day,
the meditation room, or else a tower
        in which to tune up bardo power
provides a sanctuary for work and play
        or balletic sex by the hour
with groupies hanging out, just for a lay.

        Timothy's mind
directs the show, like he's on a spaceship,
        the module letting rip
across the neural galaxies to find
        consciousness is the solar blip
to which all cosmic energies respond.

        Taking time out
is what they do, this stoned community
        intent on being free
of every binding statutory threat.
        They live in harmony
certain that peace is what it's all about.

CALIFORNIA
DREAMING

Ultimate Spinach

The crowd assembles in the dusty sun,
a field of stoned alumni to a sound
dispersed across the territory it's won.

The quartet tune, cello, keyboards, guitar,
their melodies shape-shift like mist, the near
panning through amps, as though it's travelled far.

The band interpret their peculiar drug,
LSD's coloured patterns, and the air
grows patchy with the increase of white fog.

Their sound stretches the mind to breaking point,
goes out on a long curved trajectory:
the singer pauses to refresh a joint.

They scale down to Gregorian harmonies,
waltz tempos cutting into hard rock lines:
grape bunches of red balloons hang in the trees.

Everyone's turning to atomized light,
photons for brain cells, stardust energies,
a unit opting for collective flight—

a dancy, choreographed levity.
The band pitch 'Mind Flowers' to overkill;
the fog structures its own anatomy.

A bonfire's lit, a racy orange cone
that feeds the gathered. There's a hologram
raying out from the singer's collarbone.

The stage is lost in white Pacific smoke,
the music firing from an opaque screen
returns from virtuoso to the hook.

Players and crowd connect invisibly
around a pulsing centre. Nothing's lost.
They come together in one chemistry.

Jefferson Airplane

Anthemic, high on summer's histamine,
they're outdoors playing chamber music loud,
strolling their tempo in delayed sunshine.

They're grassy unrehearsed perfectionists
opening the afternoon out like a rose
in all its heady involuted twists.

They start to build on sound with attitude,
upping the volume, while the crowd adjust
to chords instructing variants of mood.

'White Rabbit''s their surrealist crowd-pleaser,
upended lyrics and fuzzy guitar,
a storm channelled through the pilled-up singer

who dances disembodied, all wild hair.
Couples are naked. Boundaries disappear.
A hawk wheels over in the clear blue air.

They're on the Carmel coast, light and shadow
in equal mix are plotted on the field.
The music somersaults from fast to slow.

Cypress and pine measure out solid shade
in dark blue tangents, or create a pool.
Somebody sits there, bad-tripping, afraid

he'll be swallowed through a wormhole in space.
A biker checks the scene, a Hell's Angel,
a green tattoo like spinach on his face.

The crowd throws flowers. Blue smoke cooked like rope
circulates with its acrid density
distilled by raw constituents of dope.

The Grateful Dead

They're family at the Fillmore, rootier
than Robert Johnson, spacier
than Dylan's urban eschatology,
heavier than a Grand Prix pits,
lysergic as the bloodshot-eyed snowflakes

reddening under the tomato dawn.
Their set is epic, it bends notes
around the universe.
Time disappears: each number opens out
like a river discovering the sea

as they tool 'Dark Star' to improvised warp,
so West Coast Homeric its legendary.
Their dealer, Super Spade dispenses trips
to the front rows, the aisles are fogged by hash—
a thick swathe like a saucer-shaped UFO.

The Deadheads flesh out the anatomy
of bluegrass chestnuts flashed by acid rock,
the myth cooking inside the chemistry.
Shaped by the music, they're its carriers,
like chlorophyll conversion by a tree.

Those Fillmore nights they do acoustic too—
'Dire Wolf', 'High time', 'Black Peter' as a run,
a mellowing like the fade in a leaf
from green to orange, but recombinant
in grouping to a funkier attack.

The music builds by its own invention,
rattlesnake Pete Green inflecting a weave
into the pattern, as the light-show nukes
collisional asteroids on a screen,
the colours showing purple, red and green.

Garcia hitches counterpoint to bass,
the music travels on a cosmic arc.
Somebody patches a tape to soundboard,
archives their retrieval, and hours later
dubs the first for a friend and mails abroad.

The Man

The light codes in photons all afternoon,
rays from big planets atomised
as chromosomes in Acid Joe's

druggily optimistic cells.
He deals to heads at Monterey,
vision that comes up purple in clean analogue,

you'll see yourself a pupal moth
kitted to fly, red sun-spots on gold wings
opening out along the spine.

Joe moves from group to group, a buckskin god
to the collective, dispensing
gateways to altered states, transparency

to mind-read patterns, tunnels in back-brain.
He's like a messenger come out of hills
with god-shaped chemicals

inside a moleskin pouch.
Hendrix tunes backstage, each tormented chord
sounding like it belongs to aerospace,

jet-whine turboed in a hangar.
The night comes on as blueness deepening
to loss of neighbouring outline,

fires speaking tongues for solidarity.
Joe trips through grey soupy uncertainties
to some place where he's clear again,

the brightness at him in a steady pour.
The crush begins, speakers rolling thunder
for Jimi's onstage rocket-fuelled payload,

his left arm wheeling like a force
staying a car at 90mph on a mountain road,
the wah-wah squealing like brakes jammed on hold.

California Dreaming

Gram Parsons picks a blue-grass chord,
shapes it like a wild meadow flower
saxifrage or angelica

seeded by a ruby-tipped humming-bird.
The wind at Santa Ana spins
a word articulating emptiness,

then snags like a kite meshed in trees.
The canyons echo with an urgent bike
snarlish the way a chainsaw bites

a clean orange circular groove.
Fear's in the air. Men ride out of the sun
and leave a butchered trail of autopsies.

David Crosby pits corn into a pan.
The Byrds are history: jangly, space-age rock
replaced by a roots assemblage,

walking their songs as fluently
as a chestnut mare follows for blue shade.
Death's at his back like pressure in the air.

Charlie's been to the moon; his re-entry
keeps him hallucinating in the pull
of relocated gravity.

Somebody's playing the Doors volume up
detonating from a top floor
hung over with blackout blinds.

The tone's dead level like aiming a gun:
Morrison's voice laying hands on the spine
glacial as holes punched in a frozen lake.

His maniacal voice rolls through the hills
as menace, like thunder at night
rattling the windows to smash a way in.

Expecting to Fly

The discharged GIs paranoia feeds
a vulnerability to flip
on wedgy joints.
    On Thorazine
he still sees swamp-camouflaged Vietcong
pissing rainbow parabolas

into a queasy
green-scummed pond.
He counts the dead inside him like traffic
that's always passing through
anonymous,

the ones without faces or legs or arms
staying longest
of the cast.
They're shot with holes and lesioned like the President's

grey matter.
His consolation's holding to a song,
its harmonies luscious as pink camellias
unfolding a hot cerise.

Buffalo Springfield up for play
their voices thin like mountain air,
like flight, and graduating to a point
the eye searches hearing a plane

crossing a high peak through brushed cloud.
He listens to the song's trajectory
as a redemptive resting-point
in time, three minutes omission

from flashbacks to a killing field.
He's long-haired, shaky, loaded at the bar,
and don't know who he is or why

this optional bright space appears
as a calm intermission listening

over and over to 'Expecting to Fly'.

H.P. Lovecraft

An 1811 ship's bell
spells out payback presentiments
a sonorous deep-sea swell
invading the band's gothic psych,
reed embellishments, harpsichord,
a board-rolling, marine trip
on 'The White Ship'.

Their sound's strung into 1968
like a spider's print-out
hammocked with dew-beads between leaves
in Marin County, equilibrium
maintained by spin
inside a hub
resembling the sun.

Loonily posed
for a wilderness photograph,
they group in dense eucalyptus cover
around a toppled trunk, the heat
visible on their sun-glazed skin,
(the extempore birdsong's imagined),
but real to them, in a moment

made permanent.
They're hoping music might still change
the way we are, or turn us round
to vision. Somewhere there's a light
instructive to the stratagem,
pouring behind them, screened by trees,
and equal on arrival.

Time sticks inside the photograph's
selective accidentals.
They can't move forward or back.
My guess is they went off through woods
to pick up odds and ends in time,
noting along the way a bird
or leaf-green lizard on the track.

L.A. Cults

They sit, fixated by expiring surf,
each blue Pacific wave's check-in
running a rainbow to their feet.
The Brotherhood trip to Laguna Beach,
a rogue nucleus, a family

aspiring to the visionary
gateway that opens the mind
like an orange molecular
anemone.

They ray out round the coast
and bind to other cults: the Weathermen,
Proud Eagle Tribe, the Quartermoon,
Armed-Love conspiracy, and host

community, turn to the land
as source, and deeper the interior,
the un-owned kingdoms, inner space
with its illimitable liberty

for psychoactive cosmonauts.
Stoned in the rain, they shamanise
the senses, learn the eagle's mind

as a bright point to the wind,
dream how the river is a skinless snake,
the spider the progenitor

of stars built out of sound sculptures;
and sight the raindrop as an eye
transporting info round the universe.

They're pacifists, turned militant
against the grain. Risen, in biker gangs,
they bomb installations, spike reservoirs
with LSD, canonise Charles Manson,
but stay beautiful inside, facing out
into the ultimate window—
the seamless point where sea and sky dissolve

in one cool blue, the same above, below.

Love—Forever Changes

Their sunny elation's
a metaphor
for a juggler pumping up five orange balls
into a collapsible
reassembling pretzel.
Arthur Lee digs around 'Hey Joe',
as though extracting the song from deep roots
and shaking topsoil from the leaves,
that frantic.
They're period, and their flavour's hot
as rock cremation, a raw
burn of acoustically-anchored
Byrds-inflected folk-rock, upbeat,
but still in phrases, like the wind
dropped to reflection on itself
mid-forest amongst red maples
thrashed to a Pollock canvas.
Castled in Bela Lugosi's ivied stack
in Laurel Canyon, they stare out
eponymously on their transience
in 1968, posed up
against the gap-stoned ruins.
They're local, hip along the coast,
but haemorrhage on the national charts,
too wide of mainstream to define,
too of the moment to kick in.
Forever Changes stays on air,
as four seasons mutating in each song,
moods wrapped in tonal colours, horns
interjecting quirkily.
To touch the lives of 1, then 10,
then 10,000 from beach to beach
up to the canyons, raying out
across country is to negotiate
community
    a Love family
sold on the music, waiting out
the change to end all changes by the sea
mixing its blue dreams into green and grey.

Love Hurts—Gram Parsons

Gram Parsons lines above San Andreas fault,
scouting the UFO convention's
cluster of blue mushrooming tents,
staghorn cholla, and saquaro
in flower beside prickly pear

darted at by a jabby woodpecker.
He uncaps a quart of bourbon,
the next hit kicking in raw pain,
the clear air seeming to describe
a saucer standing there.

A ufologist wades up the hill,
salutes him, pouring energies
around him glitteringly
as though the drug dispenses radiance
to every particle he sees.

Gram feeds their bonding on this height,
contact by pure telepathy;
they touch in disembodied ways,
sexless, but penetrating to
a centre that's composed of light.

He watches the man disappear
casual and slow in climbing high
towards a bivouac of friends
who seem ledged into the low sky
lucking it for a fly-over.

He's post-Byrds, Chateau Marmont legendary,
post Sweetheart of the Rodeo,
mapping his music's country roots
to dustbowl origins, toeing
a diagram with black suede boots.

He leans back. Everything's so clear,
he sees a world inside the one
his senses code, its colours too.
The wind's his pillow, molecules
so transparent, they're almost blue.

The convention's in for the night,
smoke from their campsite writing up
a white spiral calligraphy.
A tiny wren flits through the grass,
violent about its industry.

He dreams, eyes open to the sun,
and feels the grass compose patterns
for miles around, green opening out
across the universe, then sleeps
secure in a small knowledge won.

Spirit

They're dusting peaches up Topanga Way
    the blue down furring in the hand
    as ripeness, a bluish residue
    that comes off like a second skin
still charged with sunlight. They're back from the Bay

and sell-out bills at Sunset Boulevard
    and tuck into the Canyon's hum
    of slow heat lying in the grass.
    Manson comes by. He'd like to jam:
fluted convolvulus spill in the yard.

Neil Young's wooden-shacked on the mountain-top.
    A hawk takes colour from the earth,
    red-honey-terracotta-gold,
    it too shares tones with a ripe peach.
The band are in between sessions, and stop

to laze on the arresting, heady breeze.
    They're of the moment passing on
    without awareness it's an end
    to dreaming a generation
sleeps deathless in the canyon, under trees.

Twelve Dreams of Doctor Sardonicus done
    to jazzy psychedelia,
    they colour it with flourishes
    so indigenously Californian,
you hear an epoch in the hilly tone,

the urgency meshed with the pure ideal
    of youth pollinating a new
    utopia, simple as grass,
    seeding itself on the wind's back.
The music's synaesthetic, and it heals

where it instructs. They've tied their horses up
    back of Cuesta Cala Road
    and sprawl mid-meadow by a stream
    clear as the air, white asphodels
braiding with fennel on the downward slope.

They're a collective waiting to disband,
    but held together by the glue
    of acid-rock and origins,
    sit contemplating the full sun
diffusing energies across the land.

The Lizard King

Peyote, coyotes, acid-rock hops,
Morrison legendises West Coast myth—
the singer as delirious apotheosis

drunk on Rimbaud's venomous delirium,
the snotty Charlesville punk, whose words were jewels
ripped off his lacerated soles.

A leather-jeaned Dionysian,
personifying self-destruct, Jim burnt
like nails popping in a scorched log.

Each moment discontinuous
to anything but his own myth,
his twitchy body draped the microphone

like a black swan.
At Bido Lido's he crowd-surfed
into tentacular arms

sustained by Barrier Reef applause:
ran with the wolf from bar to bar,
lip split open like a pomegranate.

His voice is like someone you've heard before,
but can't pinpoint, a reminder
of raw oracle in a dream

recycled as reality.
He's like a desert-soundtrack, nerves so freaked,
he cooks on paranoia.

No-one can live that close to death
and not go over: one foot, two
in the attempt to fly...

He's the regenerative god flayed alive,
body parcelled in the hills, and the wolves
running to tear it, limb from limb.

He moves too fast; the speed kicks in all day.
He's messed up, jittery and paranoid,
the little that he has clean blown away.

CHARLIE'S HEX ON SHARON TATE

The Desert

The desert scrapes the mind like bad acid,
defecting Haight-Ashbury outlaws blow
a cyclone through the dusty heat,
fried by hallucination, burnt
by ultra-violet they bike the white strip

dazed by the wrong turn of their age,
its devolution met by Manson's call

to level insanity like a gun
at privileges, the Family
policing the hills in dune-buggies
cobbled together from junked cars.
Their harem's a diseased posse,

girls crawling at Charlie's command
for spiked sugar-cubes flipped as dice
deciding who's to kill and who's
to be the atomised target?

Manson's acoustic demos do
industry rounds, but don't catch fire.
They're flat like folksy wallpaper,
a glass-papered sub-Dylan tone

with psycho undertow.
Neil Young and Denis Wilson float
in and out of Charlie's orbit—
neighbours at Topanga Canyon,

they keep the shallow end of his obsessions.
He's psyched into the undersides
of power and death: to kill's to know
somebody that close, they step in
and double, occupy dream space
as two breathing connected by one skin.

10050 Cielo Drive;
he has the mansion mapped inside his head,
the ritzy Benedict Canyon elite
telescoped to be psychopathic meat
102 stab wounds later, dead.

Charlie Manson's Mantra

Rises on dust behind an ape-hangar chopper's
volatile roar.
Infiltrates like a free radical or carcinogen
the nation's immunity.
Chases out in the coyote's ululating
voice display.
Sleeps in the spaces between a vulture's claws
after the kill.
Has the testicular smell of a jackal
licking its shadow.
Menaces like a stream poisoned at its source
with titanium.
Comes up behind and fingerprints the nape
with Hell's Angels' insignia.
Noses the gene-soup with a crocodile's
scummed over snout.
Waits with the still of a lion listening
to a zebra's heartbeat.
Spooks the sandstone canyons like a fur-coated bee
trapped in the ear.
Is a litany like a Taramuhura
incantation.
Alerts the driver on overkill to crash
barriers to the ravine.
Is the virtual intruder talking up voices
like schizophrenia.
Adjusts notches in personality triggering
dopamine.
Works its way in like learning a poem by rote
and forgetting.
Writes its message over the Californian desert
search and destroy.
Hangs in on the noon like an audible
mirage.
Finds a grip between the chopper's tyre-treads
and the road.

Is the shatter-line from a bullet's impact
through the fontanelle.
Comes back on the listener like an insoluble Koan,
a death sutra.
Kills if you question it kills if you leave it or live
it and won't go away.

Manson Takes His Stripes From Sgt. Pepper

He jabs his fingers on a chord,
an untutored novitiate
to rocky West Coast sound,
biker's boots measuring the time
staccato on the flagstone floor.

He'd like to cut it as an act,
be iconised on Sunset Boulevard,
a rock god with a red Fender
guitar.
Two kids call him from the yard,

tousled acid-evangelists
they're sold on Lennon's lyric nod
to Lewis Carrol's upside down
middle-kingdom menagerie.
They warp on a 360 degree trip,

the music sucked into their cells.
They play him 'Lucy in the Sky',
her diamonds sparkling like the drug
in its metabolised come-up
as a prismatic cosmic eye.

He tunes into de-centred stuff,
backward tapes, loopy harmonies,
hallucinated imagery;
but chops its merit back, won't give
the work its up. He listens out,

part envious, part bitter too,
resolved to be the ultimate
assassin of their territory,
kill rock, if he can't be its king
closeted in a white mansion.

He pulls the bad eye on his friends,
freaks them out of the drug's structure
into a corner, throws a dark
fixating sneer into their eyes
as proof he's incontestable

as a desert messiah in his lair
of stolen cars cooked by the sun,
his guitar tuned into the source
that feeds him, and small turquoise beads
braiding his coarsely matted hair.

The God of Fuck

Balconied, where a morning glory snags
a loopy lifeline on scrolled ironwork,
he sits naked, staring into the sun

through mustard haze dusting Haight-Ashbury.
He's bagged a four-storey Victorian slum,
déclassé, subsided, wires ripped out stack,

recherché façade brushed with bougainvillea.
His teeny harem tribalise a floor,
hippie pashas, they're gangbang neophytes

initiated under Manson's spell
into a druggy bonded family
jackals escaped out of the underworld.

He looks out over Page to Mt. Sutro.
The summit hums: it authorises blood.
The pull's magnetic, and the need to kill

grabs him like an oracular mantra.
He toys with Owsley's colour-coded pills,
the mellow reds, edgy greens, sunshine blues,

are piezo luminescent molecules,
a god-trip crystallised for a banana-curved
journey-bender out of the universe.

His look drops to the street. A girl sashays
in leather hot pants from the driver's seat
into a courtyard mobbed by pink roses.

The hippies bond by pharmaceuticals.
Each week a new band sets up on the coast
another weird subversive frequency.

He feeds on waiting. There's a knot in time
he'll slip, releasing a pathology,
black with its hit list inventory of blood and crime.

Litany of the Dead—Manson

Killing meant community,
forming a bond on a blade
deeper than love, every twist
a marriage in the sun.
People that I'd never met
live in me as family
in San Quentin,
virtualised, like aliens
obituarised in 1969.
Once I was so solitary
girls stuck to me like flies to
a carcass.
A blood-marriage with the dead
was how I imagined love,
the harp-shaped seeds in the apple
detonated to a pattern
I'd better understand
as configuration.
A knife and gun
were my cold-bodied deities.
Now my mind's the sanctuary
for those I bonded
anonymously
as registration plates sighted
on a zippy freeway.
I took them in
and breathed them out again
as tribal.
Wolf and deer married in the kill.
Death's like piloting a dream
and staying there,
the boat tied up beside the pier,
the glittery reach of the stream
pointing to a white mansion on the hill.

Litany of the Dead—Morrison

Osiris assassinated
by a swampy black pig,
I was the one boated
in a coffin
through the Paris sewers
a graffiti tag on the lid
proclaiming sacrifice
on the way to Pere Lachaise
to be retrieved by Isis
reassembled as a myth
of bar-room excess;
a snake on the road
eating its shed skin.
Delirious on pastis
at the Deux Magots
I discoursed with Rimbaud
picked snot from his nose
ate it as a hallucinogen
and saw the rainbow bleed
colours down my spine
as electric poetry.
I was the one litanized
madness in 'The End',
pathologized obsessions
by shattering my mind
like a glass thrown at the wall
to crash as scintilla.
Death by heroin
meant simply shutting down
with consciousness intact
like a pilot's black box.
Subterranean rivers
nosed me to my sister,
deep in the city's veins
I crawled out on a ledge
to be reconstructed,
sewn up and set loose again,
hunting my own legend
or waiting by the station
for someone in the rain.

GIMME SHELTER

Trout Fishing in America

A rainbow trout black-holes a sunning fly,
a lippy grab from throat to gut,
then takes off downstream, bullet-nosed missile

browsing for random pick-offs, genocide
to vibrant insect flotillas,
winged yogis on the current's pool.

Richard Brautigan wades through gobbly mud,
warm fog noosing at Long Tom creek,
hair matted like fur beaten flat.

He picks a spot and stanchions boots.
The water's patterns are like DNA
decoded by swishy rhythm,

double helices sucked into the pour.
He falters, mind full of the Grateful Dead,
alternating with Zen haiku,

or interprets blanks like the uncarved block
of the Taoists, all potential withheld.
Big umbels flower beside him, begging names.

He feels America nudge with the flow,
as though a continent turned silk
around him standing there.

The digits on the stream are 1968:
optimism's a muscle relaxant,
a rainbow banners scarves over LA

The bridge behind him's like an angel slung
over momentum. He casts into smoke,
his fly blazing ultramarine.

He stays a while, then fogged-out, ups his gear.
His two slippery catch pound for air,
scales minting silver on the basket's weave.

Death by Water—Brian Jones

High summer, and the squat oaks chase a breeze
to sibilant, wind-chimish expiry.
He's countrified: foppish and floppily

reviewing water and its quizzed print-out
of flurried tremolos. All day the pool
goes goose-pimply under slow, churning cloud.

Water's the skin he breaks to know himself
weightlessly free, a soluble figure
dissolving down moods into buoyancy.

The scare's inside him as conspiracy:
the builders talk death threats into his nerves
as an insidious telepathy.

He's sighted as a sacrificial claim,
a generation's ritual offering
to its excesses: sex and drugs and fame.

His mind's crowded with restorative schemes,
new sounds, new band: he stretches in the sun
and for a moment sees the future blonde.

They're back again, the adversarial ones
with their bad frequencies. They stand around,
freeloaders waiting on their time to kill.

It's evening, and a lazy rose subsides,
volute tucked into red volute, the flower
aware of its peculiar entropy.

His hair's turned bleached nasturtium. He's afraid.
His in-head theatre associates death
with some involuntary pact he's made.

He dives, and smells the water's chlorine slack,
his killers roughing him: one detaches
and fastens like a double to his back.

They twin that way, one body and two skins
in a coital thrash, a stranglehold,
while others muscle in to the attack.

The floodlit water kicks. He stays on down
without resistance, turns a limp 3D,
his killers scattering divergent ways.

Breaking Up Is Hard To Do

Chaos is like a drug-coshed interlude
spent in a Russian airport lounge,
fragmented 68-69

the Stones are harnessed to a Burroughs plot
an undercover intelligence sting
worked like a retro-virus in the blood.

The music deconstructs. A fat red sun
monitors World's End, The King's Road.
London is radio-signalled to explode...

The East End's Mad Frank Mitchell and the Krays,
drivers who network substances,
feeding a hold over the band

and over Brian's stunned vulnerability.
A gun's pulled on him at Redlands,
a snouty Colt butting his frontal lobes...

He's mind-fucked into paranoid jitters,
fumbles Moroccan drums and blows a harp
defiantly on 'You Got the Silver'.

Ry Cooder's brought in for slide tricks
His bottleneck designs 'Sister Morphine'.
He jams. They tape, and later plagiarize

his eloquence. They're out of it
in the slow penumbral sunset
of a dying decade, a corona

dusting the West, the dark rising
over Olympic studios, its push
working history to continuity...

Rehearsals

A feedback turbo-whine, a Boeing roar,
their stop and start tuning's so dissonant
from an irascible plastic guitar

creating hangar noise on soundstage four,
it's like an airbase moved into the hall
with all its high-pitched engine repertoire...

Gram Parsons lines snow on an album sleeve,
a Lonnie Mack record, and fired up now
leans into the re-energised assault.

The rhythm's tight: they blast 'Little Queenie'
through twenty-five Ampeg amps, strut the song
to an impersonally self-coloured jaunt.

Jagger's sore throat gives tonsils to 'I'm Free',
his rose-coloured shirt, open to the waist,
moves with him like a wind-gathered peony.

They trainrush 'Satisfaction', muscle it
to mock-heroics, disabuse the take,
then wrong-tune 'Let it Bleed' to a dead end.

They're seriously redemptive, red-lighting
their Honky Tonk persona, working tight
at managing a phallocentric riff.

A bottle of Wild Turkey oils their licks,
loosens dimensions, and the band comes right,
mainlining power like they might explode.

They down guitars. Jagger's pink velvet cap's
a patisserie embonpoint, put on slouch
as a token they're through and top cherry.

Satan Rising (Altamont 1969)

At Altamont the crowds are packed like wheat
jostled by wind, expansive hippie wave
on repossessing wave. The racetrack's burnt:
a chassis litters debris on the grass.

December's shot with diamond: pink-sleeved fog.
Hell's Angels in their chaptered solidarity
have centre-staged their leather brotherhood,
chains, boots and pool cues, a high-handled hog...

They're unsanctioned security to bands,
a lawless, pro-Manson fraternity
boasting perverse insignias: arson,
gang-rape, kidnap and bestiality...

The crowds are drug-resistant to the cold,
some naked, as they shoulder their own heat
in dazed anticipation of the Stones,
red stage lights strobing into blue and gold,

the many a global anatomy
supported by three-hundred-thousand feet.
The Angels lead the band like criminals
on to a darkened stage and thuggishly

compete for spotlight, as custodians.
When Jagger comes on in a satin cape
he works for upfront space: the speakers roar
as though an aircraft throttled into lift...

It's 'Gimme Shelter' launched into the dark
on tetchily discordant chords provokes
a vicious flail of pool cues from the stage,
a random aimed leather-muscled attack,

sticks finding targets in the tranced-out pack.
The singer minces to a stop and start
striptease dynamic in howling reverb,
slewing into his wide-eyed satanic

embodiment, 'A man of wealth and taste,'
the sneering cookie moving in on kill,
strutting defiance, as the samba beat
translates itself into blood ritual.

Someone is knifed and trampled and the crowd
opens and closes, raising bloody fists
in protest, as the steaming Hell's Angels
hack in again—boots chinning where they hit.

The music holds up: riffs a rockier
mean cat blues crescendo, uncompromised
and in between the nervous pauses gunned
like ECT into fazed pacifists

witnessing murder with a butcher's knife.
The band coax psycho-jitters as they plot
the Boston strangler's serial appetite
to noose a stocking round a jugular,

the notes so chilly they twist in the nerves
like acupuncture pins, the climax gripped
like sacrificial death, the sixties dead,
ripped up by punishing guitars...

The Angels churn in, and the band take flight,
chasing from one decade into the next,
their helicopter lifting urgently
over the arena into black night.

Mick Taylor

Arrives like a sweet pea, dead on time,
June 9, 1969
summer coaxing sweet peas to intertwine,
a pink, a blue and red
stringy as vine.
He's gangly, thin-waisted like a decade
measuring 28"
closing like Hannibal's troops on Hyde Park,
London itself rolled into a collective joint,
a fuming heady volcano
blazing with hot euphoria,
the Stones materialising like genie
out of a psychotropic mirage.
Taylor's a tempo primo
virtuoso,
his blues figures texturing shape
to 'Brown Sugar', his clean palette
comprising primaries, colours
picked up by rhythm and remixed
as urgent, feral arpeggios.
He's backgrounded, a chiaroscuro slot
in the Grand Guignol's arena,
a taciturn, undervalued maestro
at sculptural licks, denied credits
as a riff-catalyst, then hooking up
to a smack habit, heroin
as the invasive leveller,
the time-killer feeding receptor-sites
with empty plateaus, flat ennui.
He stays there, five years in that frigid space
like someone dug into the moon
inside a moon-rock shelter, then walks out
as a blues nomad, cuts solo
and disappears, sucked into a black hole.

Jagger's Dance Steps

At the Crawdaddy, Eel Pie, Ham's Yard, Ricky Tick,
he's gauchely disingenuous,
Presley-twitchy, bird-boned, jejeune
in hipsters and a thistle-grey
lambs wool crew-neck from Cecil Gee,
mouth like he's biting on a Granny Smith's
a fist-sized, acidy green
ellipsoid.
He's cross-legged, like he's bondage-tied,
invents himself from awkward tries
to a draggy autonomy
a bona fide Nancy act,
legs knotted like the upfront crowd
crushed by a shock-waved tsunami
against the stage; hysteria
slapping the walls like rowdy surf.
His hands snap out disjointedly,
his head keeps rhythm; on stubbed toes
he minces like he's foot-bandaged,
then flips into gestural striptease,
fingers splayed out, and channelling
deep Mississippi in his raw
re-hash of it beside the Thames.
Years later he's androgyny,
a stick-insect with floaty scarves,
sweating a thunderstorm on stage, a monsoon
leaving the boards peppered with holes
from a leather belt thrashed so hard
the grain looks pocked by stilettos.
He's 125lbs of hot explosive
rephrasing every black dance act
by upping the ante,
streamlining payload for the max
burn-up, fuelled by delirious thrust,
like a surfer riding a tidal wave
into a coastal town and out
on shattered rebound to a violent sea.

Winter

Ice sparkles underfoot as diamond sprays.
November, Stargroves, and a jay's
ululating apache scream

whoops from a humpbacked, rimed Cromwellian oak
roots sucking mucky history.
The band arrive in swishy knee-length furs

blowing on knuckles like a horn.
The pile is woody. 16th century halls
roomy with blocks of unused time

awaiting retrieval. They stomp indoors
Englished by their eccentric pedigree,
ballsy on tea laced with Feret Branca,

January in their veins, a new decade
coded in a snowflake's rhomboid,
a solitary pre-fall flutter

of parachuting molecules.
Mick Taylor's amp's cubed into the fireplace
for 'Sway', his molten solo heals

the edgy tensions in the room.
Mick humps into 'Cocksucker Blues',
lyrics a cottage graffito's

crude slash of queeny energies.
The Human Riff's too comatose to pick.
Bill eyes a message written on the floor.

Their sound is dirtier like temper stored
six months before it blows, a raw weather
expression patterned from the bay window

by Charlie's skins, while outside convoyed clouds
stack over Newbury and the slack air's
shaken like a domed paperweight with snow.

The Stones in the Park

A spinach-green armoured van remonstrates
at every jostle, squat chassis
rocked to a tidal swell by hands

stalling its square-faced amphibian's crawl
in jerky segues through the park.
The heat's a jacuzzi; the crowd tailbacks

into a magnetic hologram.
The light's stripped of its ozone defences.
Hell's Angels do their janitorials

with sunstroke casualties. The band
don't come up right, the rhythm's out,
arrhythmia dominating the beat

that's scrambled to unrehearsed register.
Jagger's postured Mr Fish mini-dress
feeds a dervish androgyny

into the mile-deep swarm, trees snaggily
rippling with branch-forked onlookers
got high from ceremonials

and marijuana licks.
The music's raw and undercooked,
de-centred by miragey déjà vu,

they've all known this before when dead,
a packed assembly in the underworld,
instructors waiting on a bridge.

They play for Brian's absence in the park,
and how he's amongst the white butterflies
released like petals on the wind.

The music drags. They keep the lost one near
in heat-shimmer as an obituarised
dispersal, lifted up towards the sun.

Miami 1969

Black marble bath tubs at the Colonnades.
The wind's a sonic frisbee stripping palms
in cold
    so zero it's solid.
The dawn when it fires up is red and gold.

They're eight hours late. Palm Beach is quagmired mud.
Their helicopter bops into the squall,
    hangs dead,
    buggishly oscillates,
its position lights twinkle green and red.

The crowds are glued to gelled mud underfoot,
like survivors of a catastrophe
    who wait
    for air-freighted relief
and just hang on, although its growing late.

The band are jacketed against the cold
and tune defiantly into the wind.
    Drums crash
    as extempore intro
to a choppily skewed 'Jumping Jack Flash'.

They work to hold a centre in the storm,
strings breaking in hurt fingers and the sound
    wonky,
    inverting on itself
like some debilitated energy.

Richards in his red rhinestoned Nudie shirt
builds bluesy aural plateaus round 'Stray Cat'
    guitar
    talking a deep south dialect,
body leaned into a spotlight's blue star.

Some freakies stay angled in sleeping-bags,
toke joints, and reconnect with a love-in
    gone bad
    unity deconstructed,
or dance to 'Live with Me' but remain sad.

It's 'Satisfaction' builds to overload,
reverberated bass strings, percussion
    so loud
    it's like a landslide's kick-in speed
grooving a mountain through low-flying cloud.

'Street Fighting Man''s so urgent that it fries
inside the diaphragm, its directives
    that scorched
    it has the strained crowd pack
as though the rain-gunned Raceway had been torched.

They encore 'Honky Tonk Woman', squeal dead
on the hard raunchy closer. Jagger flings
    a high arc
    basket of red rose petals
over the near ones stomping in the dark.

Roll Call (1969)

A stone robber's roost in Laurel Canyon—
the valley throbbing with eucalyptus,
oaks pushing weight into a sky
dissolving blue in cloudy blue,
for clear November—the days wide as America

with slow clouds paddling in the swimming pool.
The mortuary-sized black refrigerator's
stocked with beer courtesy
of Stephen Stills.
Stone walls, stone fireplace, rustic hick.
Belmont, Steckler and Sandison

hang out as Stetsoned auxiliaries
boots up in the living room.
A Rodeo tailored Gram Parsons rakes
a Crowley Tarot pack on the sofa,
ponders the Hanging Man, then reads
a spiky letter from his father,

needy as a desert cactus.
Mick Taylor tunes in the rehearsal room,
deadheading chords so perfectly
the sound's picked up telepathically
on air-waves in Mississippi
all over the Delta.

A cougar tooth ringed in his right ear lobe,
Keith necks a bottle with gapped teeth
and does a narcoleptic freeze
on discourse, pulls his black shades down
over a death-mask, lifts a spoon
and twinkles like a hologram.

The Stones are outlaws in the hills,
gunning to storm the USA,
but for the moment seem Dionysian
leopards trooping after the fawn
through redwood canyons, buckskin gods
joined in their concupiscent play.

Myth

Backstage eyeliner's
morphed into
snake's tails

a sax honks its pedigree
bluesman's wail.
A tequila colours

to cloudy definition
red into orange
like a parrot tulip.

A guitar's brouhaha
fine-tunes a howl
like a hyena.

A make-up artist
works tone from a palette
like Francis Bacon

doing a blue.
The myth's the Dionysian
rite of regeneration,

blood on their trail
and a leopard skin coat
left behind in woods

at Tuscaloosa.
They rebirth their dead
through shape-shifting blues,

Meredith Hunter
and fugitive Brian Jones:
the gateway to power
leaving no option,
but to burn up a continent
down south to Virginia.

Death

Comes up like a bruise
on the fruit's underside; downy red peach
topped by gravity.

Mick crawls on all fours
into a spotlight's hot
tiger's eye coloured

like an Aztec sacrifice,
beats the stage with studs cobbled
to a King's Road belt,

kneels like a target—
a miked preying mantis
choreographing mania

to sophomore corybants
mouths hinged open
with glossolalia...

He's every inch a target
for a gunman's .38
polished Smith and Wesson

chamfered bullet
in orange tails and wacky
Uncle Sam top hat.

A Hell's Angel sights him
freezes on the squeeze,
let's the moment go:

'who killed the Kennedys?'
accusatively spat
out like execration

into the squally hall
Mick glowing like a peach skin
escaped its bruising fall.

About Face

Burroughs' Naked Lunch left on the stairs
at Cheyne Walk—a Panther paperback
bridging decades, junk on the map

as infiltrator to the cells,
the blue poppy as papaveracous
apotheosis

with silky hairs.
Two nights at the Lyceum as obit
to 1969—a gypsy band

pulling in players like a tribe
real estated across the globe.
Nodded off, blanked out in the hall,

tented in ratty antique mink
Marianne overhears the deal—
30 million minus her,

a band offer from Atlantic
without the junky passenger.
Keith launchpads industrial fireworks at No 3,

orange auroral explosions that burn
intense fall out asymmetry.
He shuts in with his own coterie

the weirder than Rimbaudian weird,
psychonauts orbiting a star
sighted over Chelsea Harbour.

London's tea at the Dorchester
a Jaguar across Mayfair—
a nucleus imploding on itself,

crazy as Blake's Jerusalem,
its pop re-branded and the night
coming up like the Thames swallowed the sun.

Byron and Jagger

Byron's the sex addicted bitch
his serial conquests booting up his rage:
he swipes a wine-flecked lace cuff scorchingly

at Annabella's retrousse nose,
smashes a glass to littered brilliants
across the marble floor, pulls a corner

and rips the tablecloth into her lap.
His rage keeps gaining altitude;
its rumble stratospheric.

He needs a woman backways in.
The reverse like he makes a man—
matelot-vested gondoliers

back of green deadwater canals…
He's attitude fed alcohol.
He dreams of rocking in the Parthenon,

torching the place and up in hills
de-realising into myth.
Jagger's his flash-forwarded brain-child,

the frontman camping it to stadiums,
wealthier than a Saudi sheik
or plutocratic pharaoh,

deadlier than the Reichstag,
commissars, autocrats, dictators,
he controls youth with the sneer

of a knife cutting a lemon,
dances like a revivalist
steamily possessed in the Mississippi,

recruits the media Byron lacked
stomping his dead leg through a sitting room,
glowering with cyclic mania.

The L.A. Forum '69

Jagger's Nijinsky's act-alike
a daemonic chimera
melding L'Apres Midi de la Faune
on understudied Tina Turner,
King Bitch dressed by Ossie Clark
in black off-the-shoulder,
rhinestone-belted gaucho pants
and a knee-length floaty scarf
like Isadora Duncan.
Richards' transparent guitar
kills from its infrastructure:
the virtuoso Mick Taylor
writing italics in a riff
as a detailed figure.
America's their money-trail,
jostled by weirdos, dissenters,
Black Panthers, feral
gun-threatening activists, they phrase
the lot in 'Gimme Shelter',
invoke a conspiratorial
sister from out the breaking storm,
to surf the thunder to its core.
They're hardwired to dystopian
uprisings, Jagger face-slapping
the mike like an antagonist,
their power lined to a continent
that moves with them like beginnings
of a stormy-blue tidal wave
growing from swell to a curved wall
collapsing in on final ends
in the consensus of a shattered roar.

Bowing Out

Reverse in slow-motion
like an actress bowing out
Mick slews the wicker basket
crammed with red rose petals
colour of Chateau Neuf du Pape
in a scarlet parabola
over the black Gossard C-cups
shirtless in the front row
Keith's amps like a car tunnel
right up to sonic blow-out
guitar saddled on the hip
like a lean gunslinger
directing 'Street Fighting Man'
low from the groin
as gonadal thunder
under scorching orange lights
at Madison Square Garden
the pulse jammed on danger
like a car horn stuck,
wailing from the air-bag
in a black finned crash,
the upfront with tinnitus
injected by the bash,
Mick doing his Nijinsky
behind a red storm
of migrating scallops
in a suspended arc
the band unplugging
and bolting for their lives,
demythicised in that instant
of panicky dispersal,
cheetah it backstage
out to a tanky limo,
the bodyguards like bulwarks
cemented to a dock,
the car blinding in zigzags
of rage without a muffler
irascibly hairpinning
a right-angled block.

Sugar and Spice

Time's like a perky orange
to be squeezed of its info,
decoded like DNA junk
for gene referentials:
each generation
hacks at the neural tree,
gets thrown out of the precinct—
Woodstock, Haight-Ashbury
or the Stones in the park
gunning tracks at the trees
royal oaks stationed
with scorched knotty antlers
standing like custodians
of the urban migration
to a grilled Hyde Park.
Jagger in a white dress
de-genders machismo
fellates the mike
struts in stripper's heels…
Cut the age from its skin,
the tissue reassembles
the track marks rubbed clean
like disinformation;
the 1960s soup
infected by toxins,
ideals blown out like tyres
on heavy metal roads;
but for a summer afternoon
belief's mapped in the music,
a wonky 'Honky Tonk Woman'
scrambled like garage,
most of London emptied
by the gravitational pull
to Jagger's sassy preening
at a celebratory memorial,
Brian Jones dead, and time standing still,
his killers in the crowd?
watching the trashy blissed out
rocky solar ritual.

BRAIN DAMAGE

Brain Damage
a Short History of the Pink Floyd

1

Barrett's the rock astronomer
boating the Cam's lime green spine,
wristing downriver like a water-boatman

listening to voices, his schizophrenia
big in the mix
like invasive radio.

The sky's like a temperature change on film—
50,000 miles of space
leaky with psychedelia

'Astronomy Domine'.
He jumps in the water. His red shirt swims
like a hologrammic Campari.

2

Catatonic on smack. Mandrax.
Syd sits on his orange and blue striped floor
airbrushing horizontals

indigo   cerise
green   violet

chocolate   black
orange   brown

3

A Syd-less pastoral flowchart
the extraterrestrial flyovers
are accidental as the Essex cow

mooned in the lens on Atom Heart Mother.
'Be Careful with that Axe Eugene'.
The psychopath swipe cards an artery.

4

Gilmour's the firepower on Meddle.
Where does the wind sleep? On a blue pillow.
the 4/4 tempos are soporific—

the music slow like it's a standing pool
with dragonflies pricking calligraphy
in flashy bursts that shimmer.

5

Psychonauts at the Chateau d'Herouville.
Guitars plugged into the hypothalamus
they connect to the source like a river's

digital coding. The music dreams
in spatial analogue like REM.
the clouds do fingerprints and atomise

white	cobalt
magnolia	foggy
ultramarine	red
pink	grey

6

Echoing slide. It's paranoia synthesised—
their moon trip—dark side in reverse.
Barrett's still running through a corridor

as undertow, a brain damaged psycho?
The music road-maps inner space.
It's like a river knocking at the door.

7

He's the white fridge wearing a white raincoat—
Barrett dropped in at Abbey Road
bipolar. 'Shine on you Crazy Diamond'

like thunder in the monitors.
He's radioactive, takes it at a run
out of the studio and clean disappears.
'Wish you were here'.

Led Zeppelin

Stratospherically mega-
collisional
like blues miked in the Heathrow corridor

radio-signalled to explode
in a fireball over Bron-Yr-Aur.
Their dinosauric metal grooves

create the stillness of Tu Fu's
ideogrammatic brushstrokes
calligraphizing saki blues

in AD 750.
Page's narcoleptic riffs
connect with the T'ang dynasty,

Li Po bubbling with opium paste
mid-river, his embonpoint poetry
toeing a pink ballet shoe

directly at the Yangtse moon.
'Dazed and Confused' is sonic cosh,
'Stairway to Heaven' progresses through chords

Dantean empyrea.
I'm all attention listening 1 to 111—
a Zep stockpile like WMD

re-mastered for domestic trials.
'Communication Breakdown' rips
viscerally like hara-kiri.

I throw the door open on snapdragons,
their ruby lobes loaded with rain,
the music building back of me

and at its centre a calm lake
on which a Chinese poet sat his boat
and wrote of absolute serenity.

POSTCRIPT:
TROPICAL DISEASE
1970s

Saturnalia (1970)

A limo cortège musters into town,
    buffed chrome and polished hoods,
a mobile occult lodge, bad blood
    profiled with chemicals, they cook
        a mood now up, now down,
        pre-warned a contract's taken out

to liquidate the Glimmer twins on stage.
    Tequila's like an Aztec
sacrifice, frying raw tracks
    across the liver, gummy scent
        Richards shares with his entourage
        the empty wrested from the car

to shatter as a bright impacted star.
    He's a rock legionnaire
back from the badlands with a flair
    for H, an intravenous binge
        having him sleepwalk out so far
        he's a dead planet invader

a revenant engaged in ju-jitsu
    with a Marshall guitar.
Jagger's the sun-up avatar
    louche bacchante with a .38
        he gangsters in his coat, its blue
        precisional snout like a Dobermann's.

Their hotel floor's a pansexual coven
    convened by a weird coterie
feeding like a sea anemone
    on the band's undertow.
        They talk of Chelsea, London rain,
        girls in their strappy bijou shoes,

the King's Road and trompe l'oeil collectibles.
    They're Philadelphia and its war
on stage pumping 'Brown Sugar'
    to high octane energy
        the riot gunned by decibels
        and a pig's liver thrown on to the stage.

They hex a continent by playing mean
    Crowley's aficionados
combining caviar with snow,
    faces frozen like petroglyphs
        presided over by a queen
        in cerise satin. When they theme it slow

they're sad like rain falling through a deep wood
    at night, a melancholy
refrain invasively
    speaking of loss and common pain
        and that deep river in the blood
        putting a narrative to every hurt.

Down South they recruit a seraglio
    like arranging a cornucopia
for a flesh-eating emperor
    hallucinating on mescal
        in a hothouse San Diego
        before throwing TVs from the tenth floor.

They leave a devastated trail. From West
    to East they face the rising sun
like samurai saluting its red cone;
    warlords guarded by hoi polloi
        hardwired into what they do best,
        they keep on riding, knowing that they've won.

Farewell Tour 1971

Tequila sunrise. O.J.
grenadine and cactus liquor
backstage, burns in the viscera,

skews the tempo on 'Brown Sugar'.
They've outgrown the British circuit,
awkward with their past, the damage

done by hedonistic rampage.
Shambolic in the North, Richards
travels with his own Gestapo,

he's so out of time, the drummer
can't catch up until the end.
Something's changed. It's not Mick Taylor's

resourceful arpeggios,
it's a first move towards stadia
and impersonal rock aerobics.

'Midnight Rambler' gets a rethink,
'Wild Horses' turns a slow corner,
stripped and transparently poignant.

Leeds, Liverpool, Bristol, Glasgow,
their skunk-trail marks its territory
as slashed ammoniac solvents…

London's their extravaganza,
two nights under the Roundhouse rotunda,
out of sync except for Jagger's

furiously rotating bum
cupped in Mr Fish pink satin
encoring 'Street fighting Man'…

Tropical Disease

The drug's a muddy undertow—
smack in the Tropical Disease sessions,
insidious, 6000 pounds
per half kilo
delivered to Keith's Nellcote pharmacy—

a Med locus, that shimmery
the sea cuts diamonds at the door.
The basement's hashed to foggy soup,
the stoned and a blood-sipping entourage
shattered across the cellar floor,

disjointed jams, disunity;
Jagger waiting like a tarantula
to inject poison in the song,
rushing his words like Slim Harpo
into a bluesy slurred scramble—

the meaning buried in the mix.
They're high and low
like hot and cold
no homeostasis in the blood.
The songs are dug out of malarial mud

rough, steamy and degenerate.
The 70s hang cryogenically
suspended, they're still 60s time,
apocalyptic flashbacks atomised
as residual fall out,

a band at thirty, exiled, burnt,
under continuous death threat
post-Altamont, displaced expatriates
ripping through its cultural gamut
in the near stultifying heat,

their dirty sound indicative
of a decade's tarnish, like grime
filmed on a black three tonnes Bentley,
their process a pre-punk up yours
indigenous notoriety—

Exile on Main Street chopped up raw
on squalid nights—the menu blues
and a crisp Chablis—sing a song
and go back to a seafood plate
to nibble at a lobster's claw.

Villefranche

Clobbered with lobster pots, a fishing boat
trails out of harbour, a swishy mare's tail
of fuming bubbles throttled to a V,

the beaked prow bouncing as it slices chop.
A gypsified Keith Richards flops in shade,
the water bed rolling like he's at sea,

glasses trained on a battleship's gun stacks,
anchored deep water in the grainy haze,
its crew drug-stashed with opium and hash…

He marks fleet-visitations in a book.
His parrot glowers like an orange firework
cascading into molten blue and green.

He's waiting for an E-type from Marseilles,
the Mafia dealer trafficking pure Thai
cotton candy—a pink-sheened heroin

he pays for with brick-sized bundles of notes.
It's gold dust to his cells, cool alchemy,
a chilly euphoric oblivion

like having a cold bulb on in the brain.
His dogs gorge pheasant on the balcony.
He's like an effete Baudelairean king,

the one whose blood is green syrupy ooze,
and who grows bored waiting for the next fix:
nothing entices, dogs, music or sex,

only anticipation of the caché
he'll grade by snorting through a rolled bank note,
then count the rest out like he's swatting flies.

The Big Freeze (1972)

At Ocho Rios
Rastas toking ganja
cigars sedate Keith with burru

hypnotics played at his villa,
while the band at Terra Nova
pick at curried goat and akee,

like the menu's spicy voodoo.
Camaraderie's gone missing,
Keith's dysfunctionally bi-located,

face pinched like a death's head ring
grooved to an abraded finger.
He's defected as co-leader

of his nomadic
rock mercenaries. He's Napoleon;
his incommunication vatic:

the Caribbean turned to ice
each time he withdraws, a green jewel
signposted with cryptic lyrics.

Jagger's the modus operandi,
the genus locus of a studio
scored with bullet holes from cartels

scorch marks peppering the walls.
Business as usual is his role,
shaping miasmatic vocals.

Keith's principate of St Anne parish,
his stake of Jamaica's panorama's
like Napoleon's at Elba,

his exile deepening, like the sea
deleting tidemarks, jumbling up the coast
and repositioning what it sets free.

MY GENERATION

My Generation

A generation dies: its legends gone,
    dispersed, or ageing down the years
as guitar heroes framed by grainy light,
    survivors building up arrears
of liver damage, browsing on the lip
    of old age, like rainy day carp
nudging the surface, before taking flight
    back to baronial interiors.
Their riffs are mythic, axe-men who burnt chord
    into the sonic stratosphere;
Beck, Clapton, Hendrix, Townshend, Jimmy Page,
    feedback and hot lick avatars
demystified, but not demythicised
    by time, and how it superannuates
the moment before its laid down.
    Decades roll through a cloudy arch
and disappear, like summer on a beach
    at seventeen, the greenish sky
seeming to keep an appointment with youth
    a permanent, optimal high,
big as the idea of space, and charged
    by music 'My Generation',
before September's fast scattershot rain
    shatters the beach community,
the skyline egg-whisked to turbulent white,
    the season wiped like data
in a computer crash. Something survives
    of 1964-69,
a motif linking heroes who they were
    and are as continuity,
the new gods replacing Greek archetypes,
    fingerprinting the collective
before chasing off into blowy fog
    building like candyfloss over the shore.

Their music's come to be biologised
    as info in the cells, a reservoir
of punchy energies that circulate
    as legendary repertoire.
Their limos shuffle across continents
    finning the highway's dusty roll
from stadium to stadium, a route
    that's like a slow obituary
to youth and its ideal too fast to live
    and equally too young to die.
The road goes on for ever. In the dark
    a deer runs out across the road,
and blinded, bolts for leafy sanctuary,
its life saved by spontaneous reflex.
The car restarts; it's like a glossy hearse
    scheduled for a dynastic burial
in Chicago or pharonic Memphis
    the death of rock'n'roll
in an arena pyre? the sky turned red,
    and over it all 'Purple Haze'
played as a requiem, its driving chords
    building crescendo round the blaze.

Jeremy Reed was born in Jersey, Channel Islands. Acknowledged as one of Britain's foremost poets, he has been described by Katherine Raine as "the most imaginatively gifted poet since Dylan Thomas."

He has been the recipient of major awards which include an Eric Gregory Award, the Somerset Maugham Award, and the Poetry Society European Translation prize.

'This is one great poet - as great as the rebel peers he evokes. One of the most original virtuoso voices to be heard in the poetry of our fin-de-siecle.' - *Lawrence Ferlinghetti*

'Reed's poetry is full of rich and careful writing, dense with pleasure in words that pleasure the world and waken us to its lovely surprises.' - *Seamus Heaney*

'Authentically poetic...the sort of perception which Rimbaud would have recognised.' - *Robert Nye*

'The most beautiful gorgeous outrageously brilliant poetry in the universe.' - Bjork

'Brilliant and special.' - *Marc Almond*

'A cross between Rimbaud with a PC, Max Ernst and Helmut Newton...the most imaginative writer today.' - *J.G.Ballard*

'Reed is an elegant stylist whose devotion to excess carries the reader along as he stunningly evokes life on the edge.'
- Publishers Weekly

saf publishing

www.safpublishing.com

info@safpublishing.com